Adapting Watercourse Agreements to Developments in International Law

International Water Law

Volumes published in this Brill Research Perspective are listed at *brill.com/rpwl*

Adapting Watercourse Agreements to Developments in International Law

The Case of the Itaipu Treaty

By

Maria A. Gwynn

BRILL

LEIDEN | BOSTON

This paperback book edition is simultaneously published as Volume 4 (1) 2019 in *International Water Law*, DOI:10.1163/23529369-12340013.

Library of Congress Control Number: 2019937462

Typeface for the Latin, Greek, and Cyrillic scripts: "Brill". See and download: brill.com/brill-typeface.

ISBN 978-90-04-40208-9 (paperback)
ISBN 978-90-04-40209-6 (e-book)

This book is printed on acid-free paper and produced in a sustainable manner.

Contents

To the memory of Prof. Dr. Efrain Cardozo (1906–1973), legal historian and scholar in the field of international water law, and my grandfather, Prof. Dr. Ruben Ramirez Pane (1920–2004), a senator, ambassador and one of the most forward-thinking intellectuals of his country.

Adapting Watercourse Agreements to Developments in International Law

The Case of the Itaipu Treaty

Maria A. Gwynn
University of Bonn
University of Oxford
Oxford-Princeton Global Leaders Fellow
maria.gwynn@uni-bonn.de

Abstract

The United Nations Convention on the Law of the Non-Navigational Uses of International Watercourses (UN Watercourses Convention) recommends that states apply and adapt their watercourse agreements to the provisions of the UN Watercourses Convention. To explore the advantages of abiding to crucial developments in international water law, environmental law, and climate change law, this monograph will analyze the most important hydroelectric energy treaty in the South American region, the Itaipu Treaty. The monograph will argue that adapting watercourse agreements to developments in international law provides a way to foster sustainable development for the treaty parties, the countries sharing the watercourse ecosystem, as well as the international community as a whole.

Keywords

climate change – environmental law – Itaipu Treaty – watercourse agreements – UN Watercourses Convention

Part 1: Introduction

The Itaipu Treaty (Guarani etim. 'the sounding rocks') was signed and ratified by Brazil and Paraguay in 1973. Through it, both countries agreed to jointly pursue the economic advantages that could be obtained from exploitation of the

 | DOI:10.1163/9789004402096_002

strength of their bordering Parana River — producing hydroelectric power by the construction of a dam. The Itaipu dam became the biggest hydroelectric project in the world. Today, the dam has made both countries the world's largest producers of renewable energy. It meets an important part of Brazil's electrical demands, and it far exceeds those of Paraguay. The Treaty regulates the use and consumption of the hydropower of both countries. However, due to the way the Treaty is implemented, Paraguay does not use that excess of clean and renewable energy to meet its national consumption demand. Instead, it focuses on obtaining its energy from biomass sources (burning of coal and wood). These policies have an impact on the environment, and they affect not only the two states that are party to this treaty, but also other countries in the water basin, and are of concern for the international community. The upcoming renegotiation of the Treaty can be a turning point to correct these practices; international water law will play an important role in this regard.

Parts 1 and 2 of this monograph will describe the developments of the law on international watercourses before the Itaipu Treaty entered into force in 1973. The historical context of the Itaipu Treaty, as well as regional efforts, institution building, and cooperation that helped the Itaipu endeavor, will be examined considering the status of the law of international watercourses at the time. Part 3 will briefly summarize the advancement of the law of international watercourses since that time, which led to the key framework convention, the UN Watercourses Convention of 1997.[1] Part 3 will also address related legal developments in other areas, such as those concerning environmental and climate change law.

Part 4 will look at the implementation of the Itaipu Treaty during the last half-century. The analysis will focus on how the provisions of the Treaty might affect domestic energy policies and, in this context, discuss the relationship of the implementation of the Itaipu Treaty with climate change law and the principle of equitable and reasonable utilization of international watercourses by riparian states. Part 5 will describe other state practices and consider how international tribunals have interpreted and applied the customary law and general principles of law in this area, including provisions of the UN Watercourses Convention, in two cases concerning non-navigational uses of international rivers. Based on this analysis, this part of the monograph addresses the importance of the adaptation of bilateral treaties that concern non-navigational uses of international watercourses to current international law. The conclusion argues that renegotiation of such treaties in such a way that state practices become consistent with the current international commitments regarding

1 Convention on the Law of the Non-navigational Uses of International Watercourses, 21 May 1997, entered into force 17 August 2014, art. 3 [hereinafter UN Watercourses Convention].

international water law, climate change, and environmental protection, will foster sustainable development, which is the long-thought of and well-studied recommendation for riparians laid out in the UN Watercourses Convention.

1.1 *Initial Approaches of the Law of International Watercourses*

In the first half of the twentieth century, the legal body of rules that governed international watercourses derived from the sources of international law: treaties, customary international law, general principles of law, and, as subsidiary means, judicial decisions and the teachings of most highly qualified publicists.[2] Treaties are agreements between countries that contain rights and obligations that its parties must observe. Customary international law is formed by two elements: the *corpus*, which is the repeated and uniform practice of states over time, and *opinio juris sive necessitatis*, the principle that states must find themselves bound to these practices. General principles of law are those principles accepted and recognized by the international community.[3] Equally important in establishing and developing important principles in the field are the contributions of the International Law Commission (ILC), resulting in United Nations conventions, the International Law Association, the Institute of International Law, and judgments of international tribunals. The United Nations General Assembly (UNGA) resolutions, although they are not binding, also reflect important state practices and principles.[4]

In this area of law, those practices and principles concerning the treatment of natural resources are especially relevant. Water is a natural resource, and so the principle of sovereignty over natural resources is very important for everything that follows. UNGA Resolution 626 establishes that states have the right to exploit freely natural wealth and resources.[5] UNGA Resolution 1803 on permanent sovereignty over natural resources solidifies this right by declaring that "the right of peoples and nations to permanent sovereignty over their natural wealth and resources must be exercised in the interest of their national development and of the wellbeing of the people of the state concerned."[6]

---

2 United Nations, Statute of the International Court of Justice, 18 April 1946, art. 38.

3 Note that the reference to general principles recognized by "civilized" nations in the ICJ Statute, *id.*, art. 38(1)(c), is now antiquated, and was meant at that time to distinguish it from undeveloped legal systems. *See also* comments in D. Harris and S. Sivakumaran, *Cases and Materials on International Law* (Sweet and Maxwell, 2015), at 35.

4 See S. M. A. Salman, *'Entry into Force of the UN Watercourses Convention: Why Should It Matter?'*, 31:1 International Journal of Water Resources Development (2014), 1–13.

5 General Assembly (GA) Res 626, UN GAOR, 7th Sess., Supp. No. 20, vol. 1, at 18, UN Doc. A/RES/626 (VII 1952), 'Right to exploit freely natural wealth and resources'.

6 GA Res 1803, UN GAOR, 17th Sess., Supp. No. 17, at 15, UN Doc. A/RES/1803 (XVII 1962), 'Permanent sovereignty over natural resources'; *see also* GA Res 2158, UN GAOR, 21st Sess., Supp. No. 16, at 29, UN Doc. A/RES/2158 (XXI 1966), 'Permanent sovereignty over natural

Pursuant to the sovereignty principle, every state has jurisdiction over its territory and is sovereign over its natural resources. When this resource, water, is completely captured and secured, then the state with jurisdiction over it has full sovereignty over the resource, to use and dispose of this resource. However, this jurisdiction is slightly different when the resource is shared by more than one state, as is the case for international rivers. Riparians or co-riparians are countries that have jurisdiction over the same system of international waters.

In the area of international water law, the Harmon doctrine, named after an U.S. Attorney General, was announced in 1895. It claimed that a state had exclusive control over water resources in its territory regardless of whether the rivers were international or not. However, the 'equitable apportionment' doctrine corrected the Harmon doctrine. Pursuant to the equitable apportionment doctrine, riparians are entitled to share in the use and benefits of a system of international waters on a just and reasonable basis. In the late 1950s, the determination of what is just and reasonable was established by taking into account rights arising from

> agreements, judgments and awards; lawful and beneficial uses; development of the system; extent of dependence or each riparian upon the waters; comparison of economic and social gains accruing from the various possible uses of the waters in question, to each riparian and to the entire area dependent upon the waters in question.[7]

These elements derived from a 1958 study by William Griffin for the U.S. State Department concerning the practice of the United States regarding disputes with Mexico on the Rio Grande and with Canada on the Columbia River.[8] These factors would later be revised and developed further to form the principle of equitable and reasonable use of international watercourses (see the Helsinki Rules, the UN Watercourses Convention, and the Berlin Rules below).

Harmon's view was rejected, and it became widely accepted that there is a limitation of the absolute sovereignty principle when international rivers or watercourses are concerned.[9] A riparian state has the sovereign right to make

---

resources'. For discussion on later developments on permanent sovereignty over natural resources see Section 3.2 below.

7 G. Waite, '*International Law Affecting Water Rights in the Western States*', 4:1 Land and Water Law Review (1969): 67–96, at 68, 69.

8 *See id.*, at 68.

9 International law scholars, international organizations, and state practice in the 1960s and 1970s claimed that Harmon's view of international law was incorrect. According to Griffin, even the United States early practice with regards to claims with Mexico over the Rio Grande, and with Canada, showed the support of the apportioned use of the waters. *See* Waite, *id.*,

maximum use of the part of a system of international waters within its jurisdiction, *consistent with the corresponding right of each riparian*. In other words, two or more countries can have jurisdiction over the river, and any development carried out by one country might affect the use of the same resource by another country.

Thus, there are some crucial principles for international watercourses: Further to (a) limited sovereignty, there is (b) the principle of equitable and reasonable use of international watercourses, and there is also (c) an obligation not to cause significant harm, and (d) an obligation to cooperate, which involve (e) notification and consultation for developments in the international watercourses, in order to allow the exercise these uses of watercourses in the manner indicated above. All these principles are intertwined, and their evolution has a rich history and is the result of decades of experts' work.[10]

The fact that any nation making use of the water upstream could adversely affect downstream nations sharing the resource evolved into the need for consent on any developments by the affected state (the principle of prior consultation). In order to have consultation, notification is necessary, however, early state practice referred solely to the principle of consultation. The Organization of American States' (OAS) Declaration of Montevideo of 1933 only mentioned the principle of prior consultation for developments in international watercourses,[11] and in some cases, this was also reflected in international treaties.[12]

However, both downstream and upstream riparians could be affected by developments on international rivers. Indeed, state practice relating to equitable uses on the one hand, and the obligation of no harm on the other hand, would come into tension with each other and only be resolved much later,

---

which discusses the work of Griffin in 1958, and Piper in 1967; International Law Association (ILA), Helsinki Rules on the Uses of the Waters of International Rivers, in *Report of the 52nd Conference* (Helsinki, 14–20 August 1966). For modern principles of international law *see* S. C. McCaffrey, *The Law of International Watercourses* (2nd edition, Oxford University Press, 2007); L. Caflisch, '*The Law of International Waterways and its Sources*', in R. St J. Macdonald (ed.), *Essays in Honour of Wang Tieya* (Kluwer: Martinus Nijhoff Publishers, 1994); D. Caponera, *National and International Water Law and Administration* (Kluwer Law International, 2003).

10 See S. M. A. Salman '*The United Nations Watercourse Convention Ten Years Later: Why has its Entry into Force Proven Difficult?*', 32:1 Water International (2007a): 1–15.

11 In South America, for example, all countries had agreed to the Declaration.

12 For instance, see the Treaty between Brazil and the United Kingdom concerning the Delimitation of Bordering Rivers between Brazil and British Guyana dated 22 April 1926, and corresponding Exchange of Notes dated 27 October/1 November 1932, and 15 March 1940, between the United Kingdom and Brazil, in which both parties had agreed to this position. In this situation, Brazil was a downstream nation as concerns the Amazon Basin.

following work by international institutions.[13] The understanding of the principle of consultation, however, was further clarified with the decision of the Lac Lanoux Case in 1957. The arbitral tribunal declared that consultation entailed an opportunity for the other party to object to, but not to veto, the development. Furthermore, the tribunal stated that it is then up to the parties to resolve their differences by negotiating on the issues.[14]

As for the principle of no harm, its reach may be extended from the uses of the international river to the need to preserve and protect the environment more generally, as both can affect states. Early case law dealt with this topic. In 1938 and 1941, in the Trail Smelter Case, the arbitral tribunal resolved a dispute between the United States and Canada that concerned a claim over air pollution emanating from a Canadian smelter that harmed agricultural and timber interests across the border in the United States. It also affected riparian rights over the Columbia River.[15] The tribunal established that unilateral action causing harm to another riparian creates international responsibility. The main issue addressed by the tribunal was that "no state has the right to use or permit the use of its territory in such a manner as to cause injury by fumes in or to the territory of another."[16] Furthermore, on the basis of Trail Smelter decision, the ILC sets out the fundamental principle that the "prior authorization of a state is required for activities which involve a risk of causing significant transboundary harm undertaken in its territory or otherwise under its jurisdiction or control."[17]

Regarding the contribution of international institutions to the development of international water law, Salman describes in detail the early involvement of the United Nations with international watercourses in the 1950s. Indeed, in 1959, the UNGA Resolution 1401 mentioned the legal problems relating to the use of international rivers and considered whether the subject was appropriate for codification.[18]

The International Law Association (ILA), a non-governmental organization, approved the Helsinki Rules on the Uses of the Waters of International Rivers in 1966.[19] Though the Helsinki Rules are not binding, as a treaty would be, they contained important principles contributing to international water law. Among others, the Helsinki Rules established the principle of reasonable

13 See Salman's scholarship discussed further in Part 3.1.1 of this monograph.

14 *Lake Lanoux Arbitration (France v. Spain)* (1957) 12 R.I.A.A. 281; 24 I.L.R. 101.

15 *Trail Smelter Arbitration (United States v. Canada)*, Award II 1941; 3 RIAA 1905–1982

16 *Id., at 1965*; Corfu Channel case also mentions this. See P. Birnie, A. Boyle & C. Redgwell *International Law and the Environment* (Oxford University Press, 2009) at 27.

17 See J. Crawford, *Brownlie's Principles of Public International Law* (Oxford University Press, 2012); the polluter pays principle also derives from this case.

18 Salman 2007a, *supra* note 10, at 2.

19 Helsinki Rules, *supra* note 9.

and equitable utilization. Similar to what was pointed out by Griffin's work in 1958 considering state practices, the Helsinki Rules established different factors that could be considered in this regard: a) geography of the basin; b) the hydrology of the basin; c) climate affecting the basin; d) past utilization of the waters of the basin; e) economic and social needs of each basin state; f) population dependent on waters; g) comparative costs of alternative means of satisfying the economic and social needs of each basin state; h) availability of other resources; i) the avoidance of unnecessary waste; j) practicability of compensation; and k) degree to which the need of a basin state may be satisfied, without causing substantial injury to a co-basin state. It is worth noting that under the Helsinki Rules, the no harm principle derives from the commitment of 'equitable and reasonable use' rather than from being introduced as an independent provision.

The Helsinki Rules also contain provisions for the prevention and settlement of disputes; they expressly refer to the Charter of the United Nations and its provisions for settlement of disputes through peaceful means.[20] It is in the context of preventing disputes that the Helsinki Rules state that any affected states should be notified of any developments in international watercourses, but if there is a dispute, states should seek a solution through negotiation.[21] However, in cases in which the dispute persists, it recommends that the parties use different stages for solving disputes, such as the use of a joint agency to make recommendations, mediation by a third state, or an international organization, conciliation, or submitting the dispute to an international tribunal.[22] Although the Helsinki Rules are not binding, its provisions have been accepted and used widely in state practice, and further work on the topic has taken them into account.[23]

In 1970, by UNGA Resolution 2669, the ILC was put to the task of studying all the rules concerning the law on non-navigational use of international watercourses. The resolution remarked that water is of growing importance to humanity, that water is limited, and that preservation and protection of these resources are of great concern to all nations. However, the ILC's work would take 27 years to complete.[24] It is before this work is completed, however, that

---

20 *Id.*, art. XXVII.

21 *Id.*, arts. XXIX and XXX.

22 *Id.*, arts. XXXI to XXXIV.

23 See Part 3 of this monograph.

24 The results of the work of the International Law Commission (ILC) would be drafted into a convention, the UN Watercourses Convention. The principles regarding international watercourses continued to be developed by other legal instruments. The principle of equitable and reasonable use would be in tension with the principle of no harm. Notification and exchange of information were developed further to the principle of consultation. For

the Itaipu dam project on the Parana River was pursued. Therefore, before looking into the results of the work by the ILC that led to the drafting of the most important UN Watercourses Convention, we shall first dive into how the Itaipu Treaty came about.

Part 2: The Itaipu Dam Project: Its Challenges and Advantages

The development of the Itaipu project to build a dam in South America came at a time when the task of studying the law of the non-navigational use of international watercourses was taken up by the ILC. Thus, the execution of the project was carried out while some of customary international law shifted, as will be explained below. Further, parts of the project had an influence on subsequent bilateral agreements and, equally important, the proper regional institutionalization of the water basin. There was also a sovereignty conflict over the region where the Itaipu dam would be built. All of this made the project a challenge. These issues and related challenges are discussed below, but the discussion will also include the advantages of carrying out the project, and how the latter contributed to cooperation and benefit sharing of this international watercourse.

2.1 *Sovereignty Conflict over Guaira Falls and the 1966 Acta de Yguazu Agreement*

The first challenge for developing the Itaipu project resulted from the sovereignty dispute over the region where the dam would be located: the Saltos del Guaira or Sete Quedas region.[25] The Guaira Falls region comprised seven water cataracts, the largest set of falls on the American continent, which extended inland from the Parana River towards Paraguay. It was also the most powerful point of the Parana River, with reportedly the strongest flow and volume of water on the planet.[26] To compare it with other falls in the world, the falls

a discussion of the UN Watercourses Convention and all of these principles, see Part 3 of this monograph. *See also* GA 2669, UN GAOR, 25th Sess., Supp. No. 28, at 127, UN Doc. A/RES/2669 (XXV 1970), Progressive development and codification of the rules of international law relating to international watercourses.

25 The word Salto means Falls, Salto del Guaira (Spanish) or Sete Quedas (Portuguese). Hereinafter, they are referred to as the Guaira Falls.

26 E. Debernardi, *Apuntes para la Historia Política de Itaipu* (Editorial Grafica Continua, 1996); F. B. Costantini '*Itaipu y Yacyreta como Entidades, Sociedades o Corporaciones Publicas Internacionales*' Revista UCA (2007):619–648.

in this region transported twice the volume and were twice the strength of Niagara Falls and carried 12 times more volume than Victoria Falls.[27]

Both Brazil and Paraguay carried out technical studies concerning the hydraulic potential of the region. Though studies were carried out from the beginning of the twentieth century, a more material interest to use the Parana River for hydropower emerged in the 1950s.[28] In 1957 Brazil and Paraguay ratified a free navigation, investment, and trade treaty.[29] Until today, it is the only treaty with investment provisions that Brazil has ever ratified with another country. It laid the groundwork for a future infrastructure and investment project, such as the Itaipu dam.

However, the area of the Guaira Falls was not fully demarcated.[30] Its demarcation derived from a historic treaty, the Peace Treaty of 1872,[31] resulting from the Triple Alliance War (Argentina, Brazil, and Uruguay against Paraguay), which determined how the winning Alliance divided the territory of Paraguay among themselves. The Parana River was set as the demarcation point of the boundary between Brazil and Paraguay. To demarcate the new territories, the Treaty established a Demarcation Commission, to be formed by representatives from both Brazil and Paraguay, and established that the demarcation should be performed in the shortest term possible.[32] In the instructions

27 'Saltos del Guaira, uno de los cuatro "paraísos perdidos"', *ABC Color* (Paraguay) (9 October 2014).

28 M. Mariotti, '*Posibilidades del Desarrollo de la Industria hidroeléctrica en el Paraguay*', I Revista de la Sociedad Científica del Paraguay (1925); G. T. Bertoni, *Geografia Económica del Paraguay* (Editorial Guarani, 1940); other references and expeditions are reproduced in L. Ramos Gimenez 'Sobre el Salto del Guaria al Oido de America', *Patria* (Asunción), 21 April 1966. In 1955, Brazil was already participating in numerous studies for economical use of the hydraulic resources in the area. *See* studies of the Comisión Interestadal de la Cuenca del Parana-Uruguay (CIBPU) 1955; Servicio de Navegación de la Cuenca del Plata (SNBP) 1958; Overseas Electrical Industry Survey Institute 1960, mentioned in Debernardi, *supra* note 26.

29 General Treaty of Trade and Investments between the Republic of the United States of Brazil and the Republic of Paraguay, entered into force 6 September 1957. Although this treaty contains investment provisions, it differs from modern versions of bilateral investment treaties in that it lacks an independent expropriation clause. Its provisions resemble more those contained in friendship, commerce and navigation treaties.

30 The Peace Treaty (Loizaga-Cotegipe), dated 9 January 1872, resulting from the Triple Alliance War (Argentina, Brazil and Uruguay against Paraguay) determined how the territory of Paraguay was divided among the winning Alliance states. The Parana River was the demarcation point of boundary between Brazil and Paraguay. However, the instructions of the Demarcation Commission regarding the Guaira Falls were not carried out.

31 Peace Treaty 1872, *id.*, art. 1; *see also* M. A. Zydan Soria, *Usina de Itaipu. Integracao Energética Entre Brasil e Paraguai* (Editora UFPR, 2012), at 56; E. Cardozo, *Los Derechos del Paraguay sobre los Saltos del Guaira* (Asunción: Talleres Gráficos, 1965), at 91.

32 Peace Treaty 1872, *id.*, art. 2; *see also* Costantini, *supra* note 26.

to demarcate the boundary line between Brazil and Paraguay there was express reference to the region of the Guaira Falls (Figure 1). The instructions stated that the boundary "[s]hall follow the highest point of the Amambay hills until it meets the Mbaracaju hills and the demarcation shall continue through the highest point until reaching the Parana river at the Salto Grande or Sete Quedas."[33] On 31 May 1872, the Brazilian representative on the Commission stated in that regard:

> The Brazilian border demarcation commission between the Empire and Paraguay, in which your excellency is Chief, will follow after the necessary deeds are concluded ... From that demarcation point the border continues through the highest of the Amambay Hills ... until where the hills finish and starts the hills of Mbaracayu ... in that tram the hills starts to divide in two branches that are extended parallelly to the east. The mixed commission will follow through the northern branch until the Parana river that goes through it producing the great fall of seven falls. Through the top of that branch runs the line that divides to what is North the territory of Brazil and South for Paraguay. Signed Manuel Francisco Correia.[34]

The Guaira Falls were considered a natural demarcation, and this was expressly mentioned in the minutes of the Joint Demarcation Commission's Conference of 30 March 1874. Between 1872 and 1874 the Joint Demarcation Commission agreed on six demarcation points.[35] Two more agreements were intended to further establish demarcation instructions, but they were both objected to by the states.[36] The meetings in which the issues of the border were discussed

33 The instructions were given to the Paraguayan representative on the Demarcation Commission. Cardozo, *supra* note 31, at 107. Translation by author.

34 Instruction of the Brazilian Demarcation Commission, 31 May 1872, First Section, Number 20. Reproduced in *Patria* (Asunción), 24 June 1966. Translation by author.

35 There was another Boundary Commission established in the year 1962. See further below.

36 Protocol of 7 January 1874. Paraguayan officials claimed that Brazil used military coercion when signing this protocol, so it was counterclaimed that it was invalid. The Complementary Treaty of Boundaries of 31 May 1927, which was claimed to be a document to rectify the unilateral alleged deficiency of the Peace Treaty 1872 provisions regarding the boundaries, was also objected to by Paraguay, which claimed that there were no deficiencies in the Peace Treaty. In 1930 there was a Protocol of Instructions for the Demarcation of the Boundary with Brazil, and it expressly maintained the 1872 Treaty provisions. The agreement was signed by Fulgencio R. Moreno representing Paraguay and Octavio Mangabeira for Brazil. *See* I. Ramirez, 'El Litigio Fronterizo con el Brasil: Desenmascaramiento de Itamarati', *Patria* (Asunción), 1966; Debernardi *supra* note 26, at 43–45.

were always made under the auspices of the Joint Demarcation Commission, which met during specific conferences, and its work lasted for decades.[37]

On 20 November 1961, at the 25th Conference of the Joint Commission held at Rio de Janeiro, it was made explicit that the demarcation should proceed and there were express instructions on how to proceed. There were aero-photographic measurements and these were described as a basis for the demarcation as they showed the respective heights of the peaks. Such measurements were also approved by the Brazilian representative. The work was carried out until 1962, with 846 demarcation points determined, 341 of which were in the heights of the hills of Mbaracayu. The last of these demarcation points, no. 341, was 20 km to the west before reaching the Guaira Falls on the Parana River. During 1962 and 1963, there were further measurements of each of these heights, which confirmed the northern peak of Guaira Falls as the highest. These topographic studies could have served as a basis for continuing with the demarcation of the remaining 20 km above Guaira Falls, as per the instructions of the 1930 Protocol to the 1872 Peace Treaty provisions in regard to demarcation.[38] However, at the following (26th) scheduled conference of the Joint Commission to be held in Asunción, the Brazilian representative did not show up. The Government of Brazil issued a note declaring the precarious state of health of its representative, Don Francisco Fontaura de Azambuja, as justification for their absence.[39] So the remaining demarcations in the region of Guaira Falls as per the instructions were not finalized.

The plans for the Itaipu project are relevant in this regard. While these Joint Boundary Commission conferences were taking place, in the late 1950s Brazil carried out technical works in the area of the Guaira Falls unilaterally.[40]

---

37 The Commission met on the following occasions: At the 2nd Conference of 29 July 1933; 11th Conference of 21 August 1939; 13th Conference of 5 May 1941; 15th Conference of 29 May 1945; and the 21st Conference of 21 December 1955. More precise demarcations only started with the work of the Joint Border Paraguayan-Brazilian Commission in 1945. These meetings are recorded in Minutes of the Meetings under the respective years, in Historical Archives, Foreign Affairs Ministry, Paraguay; meetings also mentioned in J. Blanc, '*Itaipu's Forgotten History: The 1965 Brazil-Paraguay Border Crisis and the New Geopolitics of the Southern Cone*', 50 Journal of Latin American Studies (2017): 383–409.

38 Aero-photographic metric performed by the Geography Service of Rio de Janeiro in August 1959; Ramirez, *supra* note 36; Debernardi, *supra* note 26, at 43–45.

39 Debernardi, *id.*; Historical Archives, Foreign Affairs Ministry, Paraguay.

40 *See* studies of the Comisión Interestadual de la Cuenca del Parana-Uruguay (CIBPU) 1955; Servicio de Navegación de la Cuenca del Plata (SNBP) 1958; Overseas Electrical Industry Survey Institute 1960, mentioned in Debernardi, *supra* note 26.

This prompted a reaction on the Paraguayan side in 1962, around the same time as the absence of the Brazilian representative at the Joint Demarcation Commission conference. In 1962, the Paraguayan Foreign Affairs Minister, Raul Sapena Pastor, officially complained to Brazil that it could not unilaterally decide on a project involving the construction of a dam in the area because that region was exclusive part of Paraguay's territory.[41] Brazil disputed this. Between 1962 and 1965 diplomatic notes between the two countries were exchanged regarding the issue of sovereign rights in this region.[42]

In 1963, while these positions were still being debated by the two countries, the Brazilian Energy Minister, Oliveira Brito, and representatives of the Brazilian public electricity company Eletrobras and specialized energy institutions visited Paraguay.[43] They presented to the Paraguayan government an analysis of the energy potential, together with projects of how this potential of the region could be exploited. In 1964, the presidents of both countries met to discuss this endeavor.[44] The focus of the discussion between the two countries shifted from conflict over demarcations to the economic advantages that could be obtained from the river. Brazil, however, soon thereafter faced a coup, and the president and its government and politics changed.[45] Following this, in 1965, Brazil escalated the dispute by establishing a military presence in the area of Guaira Falls, a situation that agitated Paraguay.[46] The Paraguayan Foreign Affairs Minister protested against these actions. Brazil proceeded by founding a port in the area.[47]

---

41 Cardozo, *supra* note 31. The complaint was sent to the Brazilian Foreign Affairs Minister, Francisco Clementino de Santhiago Dantas on 12 March 1962. *See* Debernardi *supra* note 26, at 48.

42 *See* Cardozo, *supra* note 31, and Debernardi, *supra* note 26, for details.

43 The visit took place on 2 September 1963. The participants were: from Eletrobras, the President Paulo Richer, Director Emilio Carvalho, and Counselors Tavarez de Matos and Hiram Rolim; from the Brazilian National Council on Water and Energy, President, Rogerio Teixeira Mendes; from the Energy Committee for the Centre-South Region, Coordinator Mario Lannes Cunha; and from the Brazilian Working Group of Sete Quedas, Coordinator Mario Lopes Leao and member Paulo Mendes da Rocha. *See* Debernardi, *supra* note 26, at 52.

44 Paraguayan President Alfredo Stroessner and Brazilian President Joao Goulart met at Tres Marias, in Matto Grosso, Brazil on 19 January 1964.

45 *See* Blanc, *supra* note 37.

46 The military occupation by Brazilian forces occurred in June 1965.

47 Paraguayan Foreign Affairs Office, Note Verbale DPI No. 712, 14 December 1965. The Paraguayan Foreign Affairs Office also sent a delegation comprising the Deputy Secretary of Foreign Affairs, the Legal Counsel, a member of the Boundary Demarcation Committee, and a member of the Presidential staff to verify the military occupation and with instructions to take photographs. They were arrested by the Brazilian military forces and were

Recently, Blanc has suggested that the conflict between Brazil and Paraguay came about due to different interpretations of what the region's falls consist of. Paraguay considered the seven falls (Saltos del Guaira) as belonging to one singular body of water, whereas Brazil considered each fall as a separate object to be distinguished from the others.[48] Though these different interpretations might have played a role in each country's claims, they do not reflect the main disputed issue. The Peace Treaty regarding boundary demarcations between Brazil and Paraguay, the claims over the instructions given to the Demarcation Commission deriving from what the Treaty had established, the actions of the Joint Boundary Commissions, and the *note verbale* between the two governments clearly show that the dispute concerned the sovereign rights and use of force through the military presence in the Guaira Falls area.

Paraguay's claim was based on the fact that the northern branch of the region was the higher branch, and therefore, pursuant to the Peace Treaty, the Guaira Falls were part of its national territory as per the Treaty. The Brazilian position was based on the claim that the southern branch was higher.[49] Both positions were indeed argued, but the evidence for these claims was contested. The Paraguayan government based its case on the 1962–1963 air photograph from the Joint Boundary Commission, which confirmed that the most northern fall was the highest point. The Brazilian government relied on a map from 1930 to support its claim. Paraguayan officials remarked that the original map had been tampered with by modifying the original boundary line, and that even if one considered the southern branch, the resulting sovereign rights to Brazil would start only from the fifth fall. Instead, the map that was presented by Brazilian officials brought the whole region into Brazilian territory.[50]

The Brazilian military occupation of the region of Guaira Falls internationalized the matter. On 24 November 1965, U.S. Secretary of State, Dean Rusk, briefly visited Paraguay, and on that occasion the President of Paraguay, Alfredo Stroessner, requested that he use his influence with the Brazilian government and ask them to negotiate with Paraguay with the aim of removing the Brazilian

forced to give them the photographic camera. The Paraguayan Foreign Office complained to Brazil about these actions on October 22 1965. Debernardi *supra* note 26, at 55.

48 *See* Blanc, *supra* note 37, at 388. However, Blanc gives no sources for these claims except for the main Peace Treaty. Subsequent historical documents like the boundary commission instructions and official note exchanges between the two countries and evidence like the air photograph, clearly provide a broader context than Blanc's two perspectives that are discussed above.

49 Note Verbale by Brazil's Ambassador in Asunción, Dr. Jayme de Souza Gomes, to the Paraguayan Foreign Affairs Ministry, dated 29 October 1965.

50 *See* A. Nickson, '*The Itaipu Hydro-Electric Project: The Paraguayan Perspective*', 2:1 Bulletin of Latin American Research (1982): 1–20, at 3–4; Cardozo, *supra* note 31, at 155. *See* Figure 1.

forces from the area of Guaira Falls.[51] Also, Debernardi points out that a year later, when Paraguay's Minister of Justice and Labour, Sabino Montanaro, travelled to the United States, he met again with Rusk in Washington to request that the United States mediate the conflict. Montanaro reported back that the issue of Guaira Falls worried the United States. He stated that it was made clear that the United States was interested in the parties reaching an amicable solution, and make use of the hydraulic force of the Guaira Falls. For that purpose, the United States was going to get involved through the Inter-American Development Bank (IADB) in pursuit of an amicable solution to the border problem.[52] However, from later official reports of the United States (1966–1968) it is known that the main aim of the United States at the time was to establish the Alliance for Progress initiative, and the lack of direct support for Paraguay was connected to its President, Alfredo Stroessner, whose government was seen as dictatorial.[53] However, Uruguay offered to mediate in the matter. On May 1966, a Uruguayan nation-wide newspaper stated:

> The occupation of Brazilian troops of this border region that according to the 1872 Treaty belongs to Paraguay, provokes unrest in the Latin American Foreign Affairs Ministries. The seven falls of Guaira are considered the most powerful hydroelectrical potential of Latin America. While the temperature has been rising in the spheres of government of both countries, Uruguay fosters a cooperative action among all Foreign Affairs Ministries to overcome the dispute before it assumes more severe forms.[54]

---

51 L. B. Johnson Presidential Library (United States), National Security File, Vol IV, 3/65–68; Debernardi, *supra* note 26, incorrectly states the date of this visit as May 1966.

52 The report of this meeting was published in a newspaper article, after Mr. Montanaro returned from his visit. *See La Tribuna*, 27 March 1966, transcribed in Debernardi, *supra* note 26, at 63.

53 There remarks are expressly stated in a U.S. National Security Council's communication to U.S. President Lyndon B. Johnson. *See* Memorandum from Robert M. Sayre of the National Security Council Staff to the President's Special Assistant for National Security Affairs (Bundy), L. B. Johnson Presidential Library, National Security File, Vol I, 1/64–8/68; *see also* later communications in Remarks of Welcome at the White House to President Stroessner of Paraguay, 20 March 1968; Toasts of the U.S. President and President Stroessner of Paraguay, 20 March 1968, L. B. Johnson Presidential Library, National Security File, Vol I, 1/64–8/68.

54 'Guaira: Nueva Preocupación', *Acción* (Montevideo, Uruguay), 4 May 1966, also reproduced in *Patria* (Asunción), 11 May 1966. Translated by author. *See also* 'Ecos del Conflicto Paraguayo-Brasileño', *El Debate* (Montevideo), 10 June 1966.

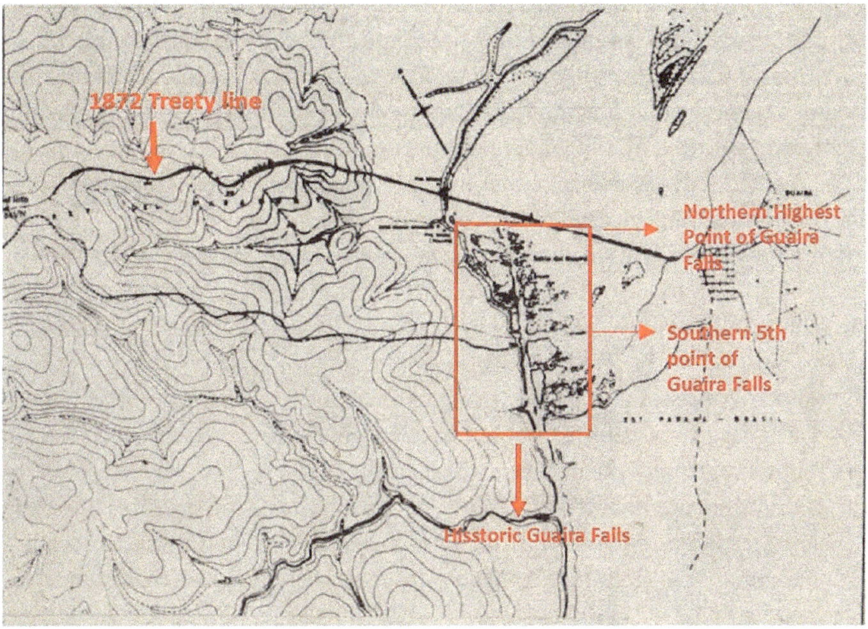

FIGURE 1 1872 Treaty border line and northern and southern points of Guaira Falls
SOURCE: OFFICIAL MAP OF THE NATIONAL BOUNDARY COMMISSION, SIGNED BY LIEUTENANT COLONEL EMILIO MEZA GUERRERO, PARAGUAYAN DELEGATE IN THE JOINT BOUNDARY COMMISSION. INCORPORATED WITH RESULTS FROM THE 25TH CONFERENCE JOINT BOUNDARY COMMISSION 1961 (AND RELATED WORKS PERFORMED 1962–1963). ADDITIONS IN RED BY AUTHOR

In 1966, Brazil once again tried to convince Paraguay to change the focus from the military occupation of a non-demarcated zone, which Paraguay claimed was theirs, back to the economic exploitation of the river.[55] This was important, as the benefits resulting from hydraulic exploitation of the river would be shared equally, given the joint rights of both countries concerning the area. In the same year, the Brazilian government changed, and a new Foreign Affairs Minister was appointed, Juracy Magalhaes. In his memoirs, Magalhaes stated that the Paraguayan government was rejecting every proposition that would

55 Note dated 25 March 1966, issued by Brazilian Ambassador Jayme de Souza Gomes to the Foreign Affairs Ministry of Paraguay. This note only refers to the military occupation of the region. According to Brazilian sources, the region had already been occupied since the beginning of the 1950s. *See* G. I. Germani, *Expropriados Terra e Agua. O Conflito de Itaipu* (Editora da ULBRA, 2003), at 24.

be viable to Brazilian interests. Therefore, he proposed a bilateral encounter with the Paraguayan Foreign Affair Minister at the border of both countries.[56]

In June 1966, this bilateral meeting took place in Puerto Presidente Stroessner and in Foz de Yguazu. Paraguay's aim was to end the military occupation, while Brazil's aim was to come to an agreement regarding hydroelectric exploitation of the river.[57] Only years later, in 1998, after Magalhaes published his memoirs describing this meeting, did it become clear that there was an express security threat by Magalhaes to the Paraguayan minister during the negotiations in Foz do Yguazu in 1966.[58] Magalhaes reported his meeting with the Paraguayan minister as follows:

> There was a moment where we almost reached a breaking point, when the Paraguayan minister insinuated that, in the name of a supposed historic right, that treaty [the 1872 Peace Treaty] had to be revised. There, I told him with utter calm that a treaty between two countries can only be revised by another treaty, or by a war; and since Brazil is in no condition to accept a new treaty I asked him if Paraguay was in a position to promote a war.[59]

The very next day, upon receiving this threat, the agreement known as 'Acta de Yguazu' was signed.

2.1.1 The 1966 Acta de Yguazu Agreement

The impact of the above-mentioned threat is reflected in the wording of the 1966 Acta de Yguazu agreement, which in its core text places a strong emphasis

---

56 The presidents at the time were President Alfredo Stroessner (Paraguay) and President Castello Branco, after succeeding Joao Goulart through a coup (Brazil). *See also* Debernardi, *supra* note 26, at 67.

57 The Brazilian task force included the Brazilian Foreign Affairs Minister, Juracy Magalhaes, the Minister of Energy, Mario Thibaud, the President of the Brazilian electric company Furnas, John Cotrin who was regarded one of the most qualified hydroelectric engineers in Brazil, and several negotiators from the Brazilian Foreign Affairs Office. The Paraguayan delegation comprised, in addition to the Foreign Affair Minister, Sapena Pastor, mainly lawyers and no technical experts. Also participating were the Deputy Secretary of Foreign Affairs, Pedro Godinot, Legal Counselor of Foreign Affairs, Carlos Saldivar, Paraguayan Ambassador to Washington DC, Juan Plate, Members of the National Boundary Commission, Hipolito Sanchez Quell and Colonel Emilio Meza, the President of the National Boundary Commission, General Milciades Ramos, Congressmen Luis Argana and Fernando Levi Rufinelli, Chief of Staff, Hugo Saguier and other foreign affairs officials. Although these delegations were consulted, the negotiations were held privately and only between the two Foreign Affairs Ministers. In Debernardi, *supra* note 26, at 68.

58 J. Magalhaes and J. A. Gueiros, *O Último Tenente* (São Paulo: Editora Record, 1996).

59 *Id.*, at 349; *see also* J. C. Wasmosy, *Archivo Itaipu. Memorias y Documentos Inéditos* (ColorShop Estacion Grafica SRL, 2008), at 49. Translated by author.

on the desire of maintaining friendship, mutual respect, good will, and harmony between Brazil and Paraguay.[60] Brazil, by a subsequent protocol, agreed to end its military occupation and promised to eventually provide Paraguay with military aid.[61]

However, the Acta de Yguazu agreement is particularly relevant for the use of the Parana River between Brazil and Paraguay to develop hydropower. The 1966 Acta de Yguazu agreement stated that both countries had the right to "study and asses the economical possibilities, in particular of hydraulic resources, from and *inclusive* Salto del Guaira or Sete Quedas *that belong to both countries*."[62] It is the first agreement that talks about 'shared sovereignty' over the region of the Guaira Falls.

This bilateral agreement expresses conditions for the production of energy. The Acta de Yguazu states that whatever energy is produced from a dam in the river, that energy will be equally divided between the two countries. The agreement also contains a provision establishing that the country that does not use all of its share of energy would give the other partner a *preferential* right to buy the remaining energy. Pursuant to this, the Acta de Yguazu expressly mentions the establishment of a 'fair price' for the energy that would be shared with the other party. In any event, the 1966 Acta de Yguazu, which provided for shared sovereignty over the hydroelectric potential of Guaira Falls and equal property rights over the hydroelectric power that the Falls might produce, made way for the parties to establish, in 1967, a new Brazil-Paraguay Technical Mixed Commission to perform further work on the endeavor of establishing a hydropower energy project between the two countries (the Itaipu project).

2.2 *The Impact of the Itaipu Project on the Development of Customary International Water Law*

Part 1 above mentioned how state practices regarded the limited sovereignty over shared international watercourses. The equitable and reasonable uses of international rivers and consultations processes (though no veto) to prevent harm formed part of customary international law. In what way were these state practices affected by the development of the Itaipu project?

---

60 Acta de Foz de Yguazu, 22 June 1966. Signed by Paraguayan Foreign Affairs Minister Raul Sapena and Brazilian Foreign Affairs Minister Juracy Magalhaes. Translated by author. Article 1 states that "the two Foreign Affairs Ministers agree to reaffirm the traditional friendship between the two brotherly countries, a friendship founded on mutual respect and that constitute the indestructible basis for relationships between the two countries."

61 However, Brazil did not withdraw its military presence, which led the Paraguayan Foreign Affairs Ministry to use the forum of the next UN General Assembly to denounce this protocol. *See* Blanc, *supra* note 37, at 407.

62 Acta de Foz de Yguazu, *supra* note 60, art. 3 Translated by author. Emphasis added.

Developments of projects on the Parana River also affect other countries in the region. In the case of the Parana River, Brazil is an upstream nation, and Paraguay and Argentina are downstream nations. Considering the construction of a hydropower project, Argentina, potentially affected, complained about such developments on the Parana River.[63]

As mentioned above, the OAS Declaration of Montevideo of 1933 contained the principle of prior consultation for developments in international rivers that would affect other states. Brazil originally agreed with this, however, in order to carry out the Itaipu project, Brazil changed its position with regard to the resulting uses of international rivers and claimed that its prior position, adopted in 1932 and 1933, had been a mistake.[64]

Instead, Brazil adopted the Harmon doctrine, even though international law scholars, international organizations, and state practice in the 1960s and 1970s claimed that Harmon's view of international law was incorrect.[65] Brazil, however, defended its position vehemently. Further to Argentina's complaints, Brazil adopted the view that it had complete sovereignty over the portion of the river in its jurisdiction, despite it being an international river. Furthermore, Brazil retained the position that it is up to the country using the water in its jurisdiction to judge whether significant damage was being done, but only in regard to the other country sharing the sovereignty over the river where the water resource would be exploited.[66] This shift was directly connected to the development of the hydropower project in the Parana River.

Argentina, in contrast, declared that for any project concerning international rivers affecting downstream nations, there should be "prior consultations."[67] It was clearly in their interest to make this argument considering their geo-

63 Historical literature addresses this issue. *See* M. R. Soares de Lima, *The Political Economy of Brazilian Foreign Policy: Nuclear Energy, Trade, and Itaipu* (Brasilia: FUNAG, 2013); J. MacDowell, *'A Politica do Brasil no Contexto de Tratado da Bacia do Prata'*, 37 Revista Brasileira de Estudos Politicos (1973): 9–21; Debernardi, *supra* note 26; Blanc, *supra* note 37.

64 MacDowell, *id.*, at 11.

65 See Griffin, 1958 and Piper 1967, cited in Waite, *supra* note 7; Helsinki Rules, *supra* note 9. Support for apportioned use was evident in U. S. practice with regard to claims by Mexico and shared waters of Rio Grande, as well as with Canada. For modern principles of international law, see the United Nations Convention on the Law of Non-Navigation Uses of International Watercourses, 21 May 1997.

66 Soares de Lima, *supra* note 63.

67 *Id.*; Waite, *supra* note 7; E. da Rosa, *'Economics, Politics, and Hydroelectric Power: The Parana River Basin'*, 18:3 *Latin American Research Review* (1983): 77–107; J. Barberis, *Los Recursos Naturales Compartidos entre Estados y el Derecho Internacional* (Madrid: Editorial Tecnos, 1979), at 15–23; see also section 1.1 above on the principle of prior consultation.

graphical position on the continent. According to this position, downstream nations would be allowed to prevent spillover damages from the use of water by upstream nations. Argentina argued that it should be up to the state affected by the negative effects of river use upstream to assess damages and determine compensation. Argentina held the view of the river as an indivisible unit, regardless of the territories through which it flows.[68]

2.2.1 Cooperation and Benefit Sharing on International Watercourses: the 1969 Cuenca del Plata Treaty

Five countries have jurisdiction over the La Plata Basin, Argentina, Bolivia, Brazil, Paraguay, and Uruguay. Facing the difficult positions describe above, in 1967 at Argentina's request, these Basin states met in Buenos Aires to discuss issues concerning the La Plata Basin (Cuenca del Plata). This was a direct consequence of the sovereignty dispute over Guaira Falls between Brazil and Paraguay. A declaration by the Argentinean Congress was published which, *inter alia*, stated:

> The occupation by Brazilian troops of the region bordering Brazil and Paraguay denominated Salto del Guayra has created a border dispute that starts to worry other Latin American countries. That bordering area belongs to Paraguay according to the Treaty of 1872, and the seven falls of Guayra are considered as having the most powerful hydroelectric potential in Latin America. They are situated at the northern border of Paraguay.... After the overthrow of President Goulart, Brazilian forces have occupied the area and constructed premises at the location, aiming to stay ... Paraguay has claimed all this through diplomatic means. Days later, the Brazilian Foreign Affairs Minister, Juracy Magalhaes, affirmed before the senate of his country that the zone of dispute belongs to Brazil. Facing new Paraguayan protests, in which they reclaim possession of the falls, the Ministry of Itamaraty [the Brazilian Foreign Affairs Ministry] proposed to Paraguay the assignment of 50% of the hydroelectric energy produced from the dam to be constructed in the region, which the Brazilians call "Sete Quedas." In other words, after an act of provocation, a just claim is pretended to be silenced by alms or participation in a

68 McCaffrey (2007), *supra* note 9, at 306–307, describes this debate with the two positions regarding uses of an international river. He does not, however, discuss the relevance of Paraguay as a country with sovereignty over the Parana River, as a treaty partner with Brazil, or in the context of the location of the Itaipu project. The role of Paraguay is of key importance in understanding the uses of the Parana River.

dispossession, to buy their silence.... The conditions are in place to transform this problem, which until now has been maintained at the level of diplomatic activities between actors, which is a profound worry for the Latin American countries' foreign affairs ministries and especially for the bordering nations ...[the following principles are recalled in the declaration] ...1) defence of sovereignty, 2) non-intervention and self-determination, 3) juridical equality among states, 4) principle of peaceful settlement of disputes, and 5) universalism of relations with other countries of the world ...[The project intends to give the Executive] ... the opinion of the Deputy Chamber of Congress and make it known to them that the Brazilian attitude disregards the legitimate rights of Paraguay, and has caused profound worries in several Latin American nations, and that all the initiatives that seek concrete action to solve this dispute before frictions get aggravated are crucial to save the peace and dignity of the American states.[69]

Soon after, the Argentinian Foreign Affairs Minister, Dr. Angel Zavala Ortiz, when asked about the Argentinean position regarding the conflict concerning Guaira Falls, made explicit reference to the invitation extended to the countries of the La Plata Basin to meet in Buenos Aires to discuss these issues. He expressly stated: "I am convinced that this study [of the exploitation and utilization of the water basin] can be made, and will be of great importance to establish the possibility of assuring permanent navigation, without the current inconveniences, and to determine the works that must be performed in order to prevent floods."[70] In this regard, it is important to consider an insightful remark by Tignino, who, although she was commenting on another region of the world, is pertinent to this situation:

Benefit sharing laws and institutions strengthen inter-state cooperation and promote the inclusion of local populations in the benefits of socio-economic development. These mechanisms are not only indispensable

69 Declaration of the Deputy Chamber of Congress of Argentina, project presented by Congressmen Carlos S. Risso, Julio Antun, Carlos Alberto Cottonaro, Juan Carlos Cornejo Linares, R. Rodriguez Vigil, Jorge Alberto Simini, Abraham Abdullaja, and Carlos Rodriguez. Reproduced in 'Honda Preocupación Latinoamericana', *Patria* (Asunción), 16 June 1966. Translated by author.

70 Statement of the Argentinean Foreign Affairs Minister to the press on May 1966. Reproduced in 'Declaraciones del Doctor Zavala Ortiz', *El Pais* (Asunción), 19 May 1966.

> in the planning and implementation of dams but may also undergird regional conflict prevention.[71]

Clearly, conflict prevention was the aim of the river basin countries, when in 1969, they signed the Cuenca del Plata Treaty, with the objective of "promoting the harmonious development and physical integration of the Cuenca (basin), in areas of direct or potential influence."[72] Included among the aims stated in the Treaty were the institutionalization of the water basin, rational use of water resources, and its equitable exploitation.[73] The Cuenca del Plata Treaty created two important institutions to this effect, namely, the Intergovernmental Coordinating Committee of the Countries of the Plata Basin (CIC) in 1969, and much later, the Hydroway Intergovernmental Committee (CIH) in 1992. The latter is only concerned with navigational uses of the Paraguay and Parana Rivers. As discussed below, the CIC has had an important impact on the international law of watercourses.

2.2.2 The Intergovernmental Coordinating Committee of the Countries of the Plata Basin

The Cuenca del Plata Treaty designated the CIC as the permanent organization of the basin. The CIC is in charge of "promoting, coordinating and following the multinational actions that are aimed at the integrated development of the La Plata basin, and to provide technical and financial assistance organized with the support of international organizations that it deems necessary and to execute the decisions that the Ministers of Foreign Affairs adopt."[74]

The CIC is composed of two representatives and two deputies from each country. All actions are taken on the basis of unanimous approval. The CIC can contract, negotiate, and accept, given prior authorization from national authorities of each country, technical cooperation agreements for projects, studies, and research related to the basin when they are financed with non-reimbursable funds and transmit to the governments any offerings from international

71 M. Tignino *'Joint Infrastructure and the Sharing of Benefits in the Senegal and Niger Watershed'*, 41:6 Water International (2016): 835–850, at 847.

72 "Marco Legal e Institucional," Organization for American States (2006), https://www.oas.org/dsd/plata/legalf.htm (last accessed 14 June 2017).

73 Cuenca del Plata Treaty, 23 April 1969. See "The Treaty of the Cuenca del Plata," Intergovernmental Coordinating Committee of the Countries of the Plata Basin (CIC), http://cicplata.org/es/el-tratado-de-la-cuenca-del-plata/ (last accessed 14 June 2017).

74 *Id.*, art. 3.

or national bodies regarding its programs.[75] Pursuant to the Cuenca del Plata Treaty, the CIC Statute can be modified at any time upon consent of the five river basin countries. The CIC Statute was last modified in 2001.[76]

The CIC relevance for the development of the Itaipu project derives from a document it issued in 1971 concerning international rivers. Known as the Declaration of Asunción of 1971, it was approved and signed by the five river basin countries. The Declaration of Asunción introduced the distinction between contiguous and successive international rivers. It states that "[i]n contiguous international rivers which are under dual sovereignty, there must be a prior bilateral agreement between the riparian States before any use is made of the waters;"[77] whereas "[i]n successive international rivers, where there is no dual sovereignty, each State may use the waters in accordance with its needs provided that it causes no appreciable damage to any other State of the Basin."[78]

The Declaration of Asunción also made express statements concerning exchange of hydrological data through publications and conservation of living resources when executing permanent works on the river.[79] This was consistent with state practices regarding publication of projects to avoid any damage or harm.

The CIC, however, in the same year, also approved a document by a group of experts that stated that the Declaration of Asunción should not be applied to any stage of construction of dams, but only to the consequences derived from their operation, that is, *after* the project has become operational.[80]

The Declaration of Asunción can be compared to other water basin agreements that were concluded at this time. For example, in West Africa, the riparian states of the Senegal River adopted the Convention Concerning the Legal Status of the Senegal River and the Convention Establishing the Organization

75 Estatuto del Comité Intergubernamental Coordinador de los Países de la Cuenca del Plata (CIC Statute) (2001), ch. 3.5.

76 "Documentos: Estatuto Vigente," CIC (2016), http://cicplata.org/es/documentos/ (last accessed 14 June 2017).

77 Resolution No. 25, Declaration or Act of Asunción on the Use of International Rivers, 3 June 1971, para. 1. In *Rios y lagos internacionales* (*Utilización pare fines agricolas e industriales*), 4 ed. rev., OEA/Ser. I/VI, CIJ-75 rev. 2 (Washington, DC: Organization of American States, 1971), pp. 183–186. English version in "Legal Problems Relating to the Non-navigational Uses of International Watercourses," UN Doc. A/CN.4/274 - Supplementary Report by the Secretary-General, United Nations Yearbook of the International Law Commission, 1974, Vol. II (Part two), at 324. Parties: Argentina, Bolivia, Brazil, Paraguay, Uruguay.

78 Resolution No. 25, *id.*, para. 2.

79 *Id.*, paras. 3(a) and 7.

80 MacDowell, *supra* note 63; Barberis, *supra* note 67, at 40–45; Soares de Lima, *supra* note 63, at 358.

for the Development of the Senegal River (OMVS Convention), with the latter being signed on 11 March 1972 by Senegal, Mauritania, Mali, and Guinea.[81] The OMVS Convention was established to manage irrigation and the energy produced by the dams on the river. There are similarities in the creation of an organization to manage the water basin, but there are significant differences when compared to the CIC. For instance, the OMVS Convention requires members to give timely notification of any project on the river, which can only be executed after obtaining the approval of all member states.[82] The prior agreement rule is strengthened with the Convention on the Legal Status of the Senegal River, which contains an explicit provision that no project can be carried out without "prior approval of the contracting States."[83] As a result of this dual treaty design, Mbengue points out that "By fragmenting the substantive and procedural joint regimes applicable to the Senegal River basin, the intention of the drafters of the two 1972 treaties was to make sure that compliance with substantive obligation should be constantly supervised and scrutinized by the joint machinery of the OMVS."[84] This design "confers to the river organization the final say with respect to activities carried out within the Senegal River Basin."[85]

Further, the way that the legal regime of the Senegal River developed was quite different. Tignino refers to "[a] noteworthy feature of the governance regime of the Senegal River is its provisions for the creation of the status of 'common works'."[86] That is, in 1978, all riparians also signed a Convention

81 Convention Concerning the Legal Status of the Senegal River, 11 March 1972; Convention Establishing the Senegal River Development Organization, 11 March 1972 (OMVS Convention). Guinea acceded to the OMVS Convention much later, in 2006. *See* Tignino, *supra* note 71.

82 OMVS Convention, *id.*, art. 8; *see also* "Senegal River Basin," International Waters Governance, http://www.internationalwatersgovernance.com/senegal-river-basin.html.

83 Convention on the Legal Status of the Senegal River, *supra* note 81, art. 4.

84 M. Mbengue '*A Model for African Shared Water Resources: The Senegal River Legal System*', 23:1 Review of European Community and International Environmental Law (2014): 59–66, at 63; *see also* M. Mbengue '*The Senegal River Legal Regime and Its Contribution to the Development of the Law of International Watercourses in Africa*', in L. Boisson de Chazournes, C. Leb and M. Tignino (eds.), *International Law and Freshwater: The Multiple Challenges* (Edward Elgar, 2013).

85 Note also the differentiation that Mbegue points to in regard to the 1975 Statute of the River Uruguay, which does not contain a similar provision on prior agreement for carrying out development: when the Statute was interpreted by the ICJ in the Pulp Mills case (see further below), the Court concluded that the state initiating the plan may proceed with construction at its own risk, which in the case of the Senegal River would be different due to the existence of the explicit prior agreement provision. Mbengue (2014), *id.*, at 62.

86 Tignino, *supra* note 71, at 837.

relating to the Legal Status of Common Works, which gave joint ownership to the riparians over the works developed on the Senegal River. Further, in 1982, the countries adopted the Convention Regarding Financing Arrangements for Common Works. These works included two dams on the river, the Manantali Dam and the Diama Dam. Vicks describe them as "indivisible property of the Member States of OMVS"[87] and thereby, "[t]he Member States relinquished their sovereign control and even their ownership of the land and the river works to the OMVS."[88]

The joint ownership of works on the same river makes sense as such works will affect riparians. Tignino commented that "[u]nder the auspices of these instruments, the OMVS members put in place a unique system of interstate agencies for the management and operation of two dams on the Senegal River."[89] Godana observed, "In effect, the two dams complement one another, for even though the most essential component of the system is the Manantali Dam, the dam cannot by itself ensure the success of the integrated project … [Hence] each member State stood to benefit from the programme."[90]

However, the situation in the South American region was different. Pursuant to the Declaration of Asunción, the works on the rivers would be managed by a bilateral agreement between the riparian states with dual sovereignty over it. The Declaration was approved by all countries, including Argentina. According to MacDowell, it was the Argentinean Foreign Affair Minister who proposed calling it the Declaration of Asunción showing that he approved of it, and Brazil immediately supported this request. However, according to Soares, "[t]he fact that Argentina had subscribed to the Declaration of Asunción signaled its inability to counter increasing Brazilian influence over the three other countries in the Basin."[91]

It is important to consider the added value of the Declaration of Asunción distinction between international rivers in contiguous and successive rivers. Interpreting this distinction, Querol has argued that it was meant to be a conceptual one: successive rivers traverse one or more international boundaries and contiguous rivers are those separating the territory of two states.[92] However, international rivers can act in both capacities. For instance, consider the case of the Parana River, which the Declaration of Asunción intended to

---

87 M. J. Vick, '*The Senegal River Basin: A Retrospective and Prospective Look at the Legal Regime*', 46:211 Natural Resources Journal (2006): 211–243, at 215.

88 *Id.*

89 Tignino *supra* note 71, at 837.

90 B. Godana, *Africa's Shared Water Resources* (London: Frances Pinter Publishers, 1985), at 230.

91 Soares de Lima, *supra* note 63, at 359.

92 M. Querol, '*Freshwater Boundaries Revisited*', 1:3 International Water Law (2016): 1–89, at 3.

regulate. It runs through three countries, it forms the border between Brazil and Paraguay upstream, but it also forms the border between Argentina and Paraguay downstream, but at the same time, it runs through all three countries. Thus, following Querol's elaboration of the distinction between successive and contiguous rivers, the Parana River is both. A similar example is the Danube River, which also forms the border between countries and runs through more than one country. Thus, it is difficult to see any added value in this distinction beyond allocation of the uses of the rivers, which would enable projects such as the Itaipu project, to be carried out.

Both the CIC and the Declaration of Asunción set out important preconditions for carrying out the Itaipu project. By establishing contiguous and successive rivers, and only requiring the two countries with shared sovereignty to enter into a bilateral treaty over the uses of the river, it deviated from what the 1933 Montevideo Declaration and customary international law had established with regards to the 'prior consultation principle' of other states affected by developments on international rivers.[93] The shift of customary international law also came about not only through Brazil's announced intention to reintroduce the Harmon doctrine, but also from the sole requirement of prior notification (*of already operational projects*); this was quite a different practice from that of states with similar agreements in other parts of the world.[94] Thus, Brazil established that only the two countries with jurisdiction over *the relevant portion* of the river waters, Paraguay and Brazil, would be involved in the negotiation of the Itaipu project. Indeed, Brazil managed to exclude Argentina from all negotiations concerning the Itaipu Treaty.

Soares claimed that it was the power struggle between Brazil and Argentina that led Brazil to give something to its smaller neighbor, Paraguay.

> In the development of a regime for the common use of the Parana River, Brazil made use of a combination of rewards and coercion towards its two neighbors, Paraguay and Argentina. To establish a regime in accordance with its interests, Brazil eschewed unilateral action in the exploitation of the hydroelectric potential of the river and agreed to a joint venture with Paraguay for the production of electric power.[95]

93 *See further* MacDowell, *supra* note 63 ; Soares de Lima, *supra* note 63, at 358; "The Treaty of the Cuenca del Plata," CIC, http://cicplata.org/es/el-tratado-de-la-cuenca-del-plata/.

94 See, for example, the OMVS Convention, *supra* note 81.

95 Soares de Lima, *supra* note 63, at 349.

However, the sovereignty conflict concerning the region where the project was going to be built shows why Paraguay was included, as this region was under dispute; Paraguay saw it as its sole territory.

The Declaration of Asunción reveals another shift in the law. While the Lake Lanoux Case in 1957 found that that the rule according to which states may use international watercourses on condition of prior agreement had not been established as custom or as general principle of law, the 1971 Declaration established the requirement for a bilateral agreement concerning development in watercourses between the states with joint sovereignty over international rivers. The *Lake Lanoux* decision emphasized that consultation meant an opportunity to object, not veto. While the Itaipu project did not quite follow this parameter to enable consultation among riparians, it did have the countries' support through the institutionalization mechanism to regulate the Parana River, which allowed the project to be carried out.

More important was the support of the countries, including that of Paraguay.[96] In 1972, UNGA Resolution 2995 declared the principle of notification rather than consultation, making express reference to technical data exchanges for the purpose of avoiding significant harm, but only in "the environment of the adjacent area"; notification, however, shall not "delay or impede the programmes and projects ... of the states in whose territories such programmes are projects are carried out."[97] At the United Nations, Paraguay supported the position taken by Brazil, not Argentina.[98] The support of coun-

96 Paraguayan President Stroessner's pendulum diplomacy — swinging between Argentina and Brazil — also played a role to the benefit of Paraguay. However, this ultimately had negative consequences, for example, when Brazil realized this was happening, it stopped offering concessions to Paraguay.

97 GA Res 2995, UN GAOR, 27th Sess., Supp. No. 30, at 42, UN Doc. A/RES/2995(XXVII 1972), Co-operation between States in the field of the environment. This was viewed as a victory in Brazil because it meant that Argentina had given way to Brazil's position on the matter. Argentina denounced the resolution the following year. Soares de Lima, *supra* note 63 at 360.

98 This can be explained by numerous factors. Further to the security threat expressed by the Brazilian Foreign Affairs Minister to the Paraguayan Foreign Affairs Minister during the negotiations of the Acta de Yguazu (*supra* note 59), Paraguay, as a land-locked country, depended heavily on the use of the River Plate, which was under Argentinean jurisdiction, for economic survival. Argentina imposed extra controls and screened Paraguayan goods transported on the river, and did not adhere to the international navigation treaties common at that time. Brazil adopted a more cooperative approach towards Paraguay as the two countries agreed to and ratified bilateral treaties concerning friendship, navigation, and commerce and for technical assistance, expertise, and cultural exchanges. Further, Argentina objected to international financing of the Itaipu project by expressing their repeated objection at the United Nations and to international finance institutions; Brazil

tries, the regional institutionalization of the basin (pursuant to the Cuenca del Plata Treaty and, especially, the Declaration of Asunción), permitted the parties to come to a bilateral agreement on the non-navigation uses of the river.

In the case of the uses of the Parana River for non-navigation purposes, the dam projects were guided by bilateral treaties. These institutional decisions and agreements facilitated the entry into force of the Itaipu Treaty. With regard to Argentina, the other riparian of the Parana River, the situation was eased by having its own bilateral agreement with Paraguay. However, it was only because Paraguay had signed the Itaipu Treaty with Brazil that Argentina reconsidered the agreements that had been proposed with Paraguay since 1926 and had never been carried out.[99] After the Itaipu Treaty, Argentina signed and ratified the Yacyreta Treaty with Paraguay, which was concerned with the construction of a dam in the downstream flow of the Parana River. The Yacyreta Treaty contained similar terms to the Itaipu Treaty, but is different in that it contains financial terms more favorable to Paraguay.[100]

---

had offered Paraguay direct loans and committed to finance them. Brazil also agreed to make itself the sole guarantor of any international debt that would be acquired by the binational company, Itaipu, under the Itaipu Treaty. See further Soares de Lima, *supra* note 63.

99 Argentina and Paraguay had signed in 1926 a protocol known as the Ayala-Pueyrredon Protocol concerning the navigability of the Parana River and the use of the river for industrial purposes. Costantini, *supra* note 26, claimed that the project contemplated under the Protocol was very unfair as it established that 93 percent of the energy would be allocated to Argentina and 7 percent to Paraguay. The Protocol was never ratified. It was only much later, when Argentina could not be a part of the Itaipu Treaty that it considered embarking on a hydroelectric project with Paraguay. In 1973, with the third presidential term of Juan Peron, Argentina adopted a foreign policy with more separation from the United States and that countered Brazilian presence in the region. Argentina presented Paraguay with a treaty to build a dam and exploit the Parana River at the point of their joint jurisdiction that was modelled on the Itaipu Treaty terms. Also in 1973, at the United Nations General Assembly, Argentina called for the adoption of another resolution (UN GAOR, 28th Sess., Supp. No. 30, vol. 1, at 48, UN Doc. A/RES/3129 (XXVIII 1973)) reinstating the principle of consultation and it passed. Brazil and Paraguay voted against it. This issue continued to be debated at the UN in sessions thereafter. For example, in debate concerning the 1974 Charter of Economics Rights and Duties, the article referring to the consultation principle was rejected by Brazil. For discussion on the latter debate, *see* Soares de Lima, *supra* note 63, at 363; *see also* Barberis, *supra* note 67, at 145–166.

100 As concerns royalties and compensation, the Itaipu Treaty set a rate of US$950 GWh and the Yacyreta Treaty set a rate of US$2,998 GWh. As to why there is this difference, Debernardi claims that Paraguay was able to achieve more favorable financial terms in the Yacyreta Treaty with Argentina because it was in a superior bargaining position due to the execution of the Itaipu Treaty and thus managed to include a higher rate in the treaty with Argentina. In contrast, Da Rosa states that the more favorable terms merely came about as a result of applying the same method of price calculation, though proving

Eventually, but only after the beginning construction of the Itaipu dam, did the three riparian countries, Brazil, Paraguay and Argentina, sign a tri-partite agreement for the specific use of the Parana river for hydropower purposes, which further eased the tensions. This agreement is discussed further in Section 2.4 below.

2.3 *The Itaipu Treaty of 1973*

After the delivery of the findings of the Brazil-Paraguay Technical Mixed Commission, the Itaipu Treaty was signed and ratified by Paraguay and Brazil in 1973. With it, the construction of the Itaipu dam to produce hydro-electricity on the Parana River began.

As discussed above, development of the project was possible due to the shift in regional customary international law, manifested through Brazil's position in regard to Argentina and materialized through the 1971 Declaration of Asunción and the 1972 UNGA Resolution 2995. Indeed, both the Acta de Yguazu and the Declaration of Asunción are mentioned in the preamble of the Itaipu Treaty.

The Itaipu Treaty consists of twenty-five articles and three annexes. The main text includes the provisions regarding the agreement for building the dam, property rights to the energy produced, the constitution of the Itaipu binational entity and concession given by the states to the entity for the hydroelectric exploitation deriving from the use of that part of the Parana river, economic resources, binational jurisdiction of the entity, dispute settlement mechanisms, and other provisions regarding the parties' relations. It is complemented by three annexes: Annex A relating to the articles of agreement of the Itaipu entity, an international company created to regulate the production, distribution, and sale of energy; Annex B relating to the technical description of the project; and Annex C relating to the financial aspects, price of energy, and energy services to be provided.

There are important differences in the provisions of the Itaipu Treaty from its predecessor agreement, the Acta de Yguazu. For example, the provision in the Acta de Yguazu agreement establishes a 'fair' price to acquire the energy from the country that has excess energy, a provision that is not found in the Itaipu Treaty. Instead, the Itaipu Treaty provides a fixed price for the sale of energy, which is not based on market value.[101] Another difference was with re-

deficient precisely because of this different result. *See* Debernardi, *supra* note 26, at 345; da Rosa, *supra* note 67, at 89; *see also* Nickson, *supra* note 50, at 9.

101 Treaty between the Federative Republic of Brazil and the Republic of Paraguay for the Hydroelectric Development of the Hydraulic Resources of the Paraná River, Belonging in

gard to the clause of preferential sale. The provision was changed in the Itaipu Treaty to a third-party sale restriction clause, effectively restricting the smaller country, Paraguay, from selling the unused share of its energy 'solely' to Brazil at the established fixed price.[102] Part 4 below describes in more detail how the Treaty is implemented.

The Itaipu Treaty also established the Itaipu entity. The Treaty sets out the by-laws of this entity and provides for it to operate as an international corporation.[103] The entity is not formally incorporated under any domestic jurisdiction although it has a board of directors and shareholders. It is exempt from paying taxes and is primarily subject to the Treaty provisions.[104] Domestic legislation of either country applies to physical or legal persons in connection to the entity, taking into account the Treaty provisions.[105]

The main two shareholders of this binational entity are the majority state-owned electric utility companies Administración Nacional de Electricidad (ANDE, Paraguay) and Eletrobras (Brazil). The latter has recently changed its corporate structure; it is publicly-held and controlled by the government of Brazil but trades its shares in the Sao Paulo, New York and Madrid Stock Exchange. This binational entity Itaipu is in charge of managing and distributing all the revenues resulting from the hydroelectric energy that the dam produces. The Treaty also obliges the shareholders to acquire the energy produced, thus guaranteeing secure purchase of the energy produced. Another reason for the creation of the Itaipu binational entity is that it was then possible for the entity, rather than the states, to take out loans associated with the project and to be responsible for them.[106]

With the Itaipu Treaty ratified by both countries, the construction of the Itaipu dam on the Parana River began. The dried zone and the falls were dynamited. This allowed for the flow of the Parana River to cover the area completely. Mario Gibson Barboza, the Ambassador of Brazil to Paraguay in 1966 and then Brazilian Foreign Affairs Minister when the Itaipu Treaty was signed, stated that when the Itaipu Treaty was signed, "the disputed territory would be forcefully put under water by the dam, and so the object of dispute would

---

Condominium to the two Countries, from and including the Salto Grande de Sete Quedas or Salto de Guairá to the Mouth of the Iguaçu River, 26 April 1973, (hereinafter Itaipu Treaty). On price item see Annex C, III.

102 *Id.*, art. XIII.

103 These provisions were also expressed in the official statement of Brazil's General Consultancy Office, approved by the Brazilian President on 17 October 1978.

104 Itaipu Treaty, *supra* note 101, art. III(1).

105 *Id.*, art. XIX.

106 See Part 4 in this monograph for further details.

be eliminated; and that by this proposal [referring to the 1966 Acta de Yguazu] Itaipu was born."[107] But there is some disagreement on whether or not the border dispute actually ended.[108] Zydan Soria has argued that the modification was merely physical and not one of the border, because modification of the border would have made further negotiations impossible.[109] In fact, Article VII of the Itaipu Treaty establishes that any installation for the production of energy shall not produce variation in the boundaries between the two countries that had been established by treaties already in force.

However, what remains unchangeable are the consequences of all this. Da Rosa described the chain of events as follows: "two related historical events took place: the birth of the Itaipu Lake, the largest man-made lake, and the disappearance of the falls of Guaira or Sete Quedas, the largest waterfall in the Americas."[110] Thus, with the construction of the dam, the whole region of conflict, Guaira Falls, which had been a natural wonder with its seven falls and highest volume of water on the planet, was put entirely under water. It became entirely part of the Parana River.

2.4 *The 1979 Tri-Partite Agreement on Hydropower Uses Deriving from the Parana River*

In October 1979, Argentina, Brazil, and Paraguay came to an agreement regarding the uses of hydropower derived from the Parana River. The agreement followed two technical meetings in 1977 and two diplomatic meetings in 1978. The agreement results were stated in a *note verbale*, which is now referred to as the Tri-Partite Agreement.[111] The Tri-partite Agreement expressly mentions the two bilateral projects, Brazil-Paraguay (Itaipu) and Argentina-Paraguay

---

107 From Zydan Soria, *supra* note 31, at 66.

108 Debernardi states that there is still a region that was not covered by water and that the Itaipu entity (Itaipu Binacional) purchased it to transform it into an ecological park. Itaipu Binacional also purchased an electrical transmission tower, but the tower was on the disputed boundary. Debernardi, *supra* note 26, at 73. The Paraguayan Foreign Affairs Ministry asked the opinion of the National Council of Limits Assessment (comprising Ramiro Rodriguez Alcala, Julio Cesar Chavez, Marco Antonio Laconich and Victor Natalicio Vasconcellos) on whether the limits would be affected by the Acta de Iguazu. The Council stated that it would not, because it would keep the Parana River as a dividing line between the two jurisdictions (Note No. 1/73, 23 April 1973). Debernardi, *id.*, at 152.

109 Zydan Soria, *supra* note 31, at 70.

110 da Rosa, *supra* note 67, at 79.

111 Acuerdo Tripartito Referente al Aprovechamiento hidroeléctrico del rio Paraná, 19 October 1979. Nota Verbale No. 16/79, 19 October 1979 (Tri-Partite Agreement). For an English translation, see *Argentina, Brazil, Paraguay: Agreement on Parana River Projects*, 19 International Legal Materials (1980), at 615–617.

(Yacyreta), on the Parana River, as examples of successful cooperation pursuant to the implementation of the Cuenca del Plata Treaty.[112]

The Agreement establishes provisions for navigational and non-navigational uses of the Parana River. Regarding the non-navigation uses, it prescribes limits for maintaining the water level, so that the operation of Itaipu will not affect the waters downstream.[113] It also establishes the obligation of information exchange regarding hydrological conditions between the three countries.[114] Further, the three countries also commit to protecting the environment, fauna, flora, and quality of the water. The Agreement includes provision that any alterations by the Itaipu project affecting the waters would entail new negotiations among the three countries.

Regarding the Tri-Partite Agreement, and reminded of the legal debate between Argentina and Brazil, McCaffrey states: "Thus Argentina and Brazil were ultimately able to resolve the dispute in an amicable fashion. It is interesting to note that the very principles that were at issue in the dispute — prior notification and consultation — were enshrined in the agreement that resolved it."[115]

The Tri-partite Agreement followed the Itaipu Treaty, and it was agreed to by the three countries only after construction of the Itaipu project had already begun. In the South American and La Plata Basin region, the non-navigation uses of shared international watercourses, such as hydropower, had been regulated through bilateral treaties. The Itaipu Treaty was the most important one, and other agreements have been modelled after it.[116]

Part 3: Advancement in International Watercourses and Environmental Law

We now turn to analysis of the new international law developments that concern the non-navigation uses of international rivers, and how these might be relevant for either adapting existing treaties or consideration in future agreements. Advancements in both international watercourses law and international environmental law interact with water law. International developments and the

112 *Id.*, para. 2.

113 *Id.*, para. 5 (a), (b), and (c).

114 *Id.*, para. 5 (e).

115 McCaffrey 2007, *supra* note 9, at 307; *see also* J. Martinez Adalid '*La Controversia Argentina-Brasileña Sobre el Aprovechamiento Hidroeléctrico del Rio Paraná y el Acuerdo Tripartito de 1979*', XVII–XVIII Prudentia luris (1985–1986): 69–91.

116 For example, the Yacyreta Treaty between Argentina and Paraguay was modelled after the Itaipu Treaty.

creation of institutions in general, as well as regional developments concerning the La Plata water basin, are considered here. This brief overview will serve as a basis for the analysis of the implementation of the 1973 Itaipu Treaty that will be dealt with in Part 4.

3.1 *Advances in International Watercourses Law*

Further works on international watercourses law were elaborated in the 1980s and 1990s. In 1982, the International Law Association adopted the Rules on Water Pollution in an International Drainage Basin, and in 1986 the Rules on International Groundwaters. In 1992, the UN Economic Commission for Europe (UNECE) drafted the Convention on the Protection and Use of Transboundary Watercourses and International Lakes[117] and the Convention on the Transboundary Effects of Industrial Accidents.[118] Each of these instruments has been fruitful for the development of the law on international watercourses. However, one of the most significant developments in international water law was the 1997 UN Watercourses Convention; we shall start with an overview of this convention.

3.1.1 The 1997 UN Watercourses Convention

By 1994, the ILC completed its work on the study on international watercourses.[119] The Convention on the Law of Non-Navigation Uses of International Watercourses was adopted by the UN General Assembly on 21 May 1997. It only entered into force in 2014. This convention proposes a framework that introduces substantive and procedural aspects of international watercourses, but it is left up to riparian states to complement it with further agreements. The Convention defines "watercourse" so as to include both surface water and groundwaters (Article 2).

The Convention has general principles; the cornerstone principle is the equitable and reasonable utilization and participation of international watercourses.[120] It refers to participation that "includes both the right to utilize the watercourse and the duty to cooperate in the protection and development thereof."[121] McCaffrey argues that this involves an affirmative obligation

117 17 March 1972 (entered into force 6 October 1996) (UNECE Water Convention).

118 17 March 1972 (entered into force 19 April 2000). *See also* Protocol on Civil Liability and Compensation for Damage Caused by the Transboundary Effects of Industrial Accidents on Transboundary Waters, 21 May 2003 (not in force).

119 See GA Res 49/52, UN GAOR, 49th Sess., Suppl. No. 49, vol. 1, UN Doc. A/RES/49/52 (1994), 'Draft articles on the law of the non-navigational uses of international watercourses'.

120 UN Watercourses Convention, *supra* note 1, art. 5.

121 *Id.*, art. 5(2).

to cooperate[122] and equitable participation, which means that "States sharing an international watercourse have an affirmative obligation to cooperate in its protection and development and implicitly in its management in order to achieve and maintain a regime of equitable utilization and protection of the water course."[123]

As state practice and the Helsinki Rules have shown, the concept of 'equitable and reasonable use and participation' concerns and involves many factors. This is no different in the UN Watercourses Convention. Article 6 of the Convention states that these factors include: a) geographic, hydrographic, hydrological, climatic, ecological and other factors of natural character; b) the social and economic needs of the watercourse states concerned; c) the population dependent on the watercourse in the watercourse state; d) the effects of the use or uses of watercourses in one watercourse state on other watercourse states; e) existing and potential uses of the watercourse; f) conservation, protection, development and economy of the water resources of the watercourse and the cost of measures taken to that effect; g) the availability of alternatives, of comparable value, to a particular planned or existing use.[124]

Article 6 also recommends that countries enter into consultations if the need arises, as a form of cooperation. It also notes that all factors should be considered for reaching a conclusion on the equitable and reasonable uses, which dispenses of any form of hierarchy between factors. McCaffrey also points out that the list of factors is non-exhaustive.[125] It is particularly important that this provision reinforces the principle of no absolute sovereignty when international watercourses are concerned.

The UN Watercourses Convention also mentions the obligation not to cause significant harm.[126] Upstream countries favor the principle of equitable and reasonable use, but downstream countries tend to favor the no harm rule. Salman argues that this tension derives from a misunderstanding that only the lower stream countries will face harm; he points out that harmful effects can go both ways. Developments in the lower stream can affect upper streams

122 S. McCaffrey, '*The Contribution of the UN Convention on the Law of the Non-navigational Uses of International Watercourses*', 1:3/4 International Journal of Global Environmental Issues (2001): 250–261.

123 S. C. McCaffrey, '*International Watercourses: The UN Convention on Non-Navigational Uses of International Watercourses*', UN Lecture Series, http://legal.un.org/avl/ls/McCaffrey_IW.html# (last accessed 12 November 2018).

124 UN Watercourses Convention, *supra* note 1, art. 6.

125 S. C. McCaffrey, *The Law of International Watercourses: Non-navigational Uses* (Oxford University Press, 2001).

126 UN Watercourses Convention, *supra* note 1, art. 7.

nations.[127] Thus, the two principles must be seen as complementing each other, as pointed out by McCaffrey.[128]

By having both the equitable and reasonable use and the obligation not to cause harm principles in the Convention, scholars claimed that the Convention reached a compromise, relieving the tension between the two principles.[129] However, Article 7(2) also states that countries must "take all appropriate measures, having due regard for the provisions of articles 5 and 6, in consultation with the affected State, to eliminate or mitigate such harm and, where appropriate, to discuss the question of compensation." According to Salman, the result of analyzing these provisions is that "the prevailing view is that the convention has, like the Helsinki Rules, subordinated the obligation not to cause significant harm to the principle of equitable and reasonable utilization."[130] This is because Article 7 establishes that even when there is significant harm to another watercourse state, the state that causes it is required to take all appropriate measures, in consultation with the affected state, to eliminate or mitigate such harm, and to discuss compensation.

The Convention expresses the general obligation to cooperate. This takes the form of establishing a joint mechanism or commission and regular exchange of data and information, and notification of other riparian states of planned measures with possible significant adverse effects. As discussed above, the Convention also demands that states entering into consultations determine the different factors to be taken into account for their reasonable and equitable uses of international watercourses.

Another important aspect of the UN Watercourses Convention is its provisions on dispute settlement. Among other things, it establishes that there shall be no discrimination in granting access to judicial or other procedures to those who suffered harm (Article 32). Second, following the different stages of peaceful settlement of international disputes, it recommends that if a dispute is not

127 Salman states: "It is much less obvious, and generally not recognized, that the upstream riparians can be harmed by the potential foreclosure of their future use of water caused by the prior use and the claiming of rights by downstream riparians. For example, a poor upstream country could be precluded from developing the water resources of an international waterway tomorrow if a richer downstream riparian, without consultation or notification, develops it today." Salman 2007a, *supra* note 10, at 9. Other examples include the construction of a dam that can block navigation or affect fish migration.

128 McCaffrey 2001, *supra* note 125; McCaffrey 2007, *supra* note 9.

129 *See* Salman 2007a, *supra* note 10; McCaffrey 2007, *supra* note 9.

130 S. M. A. Salman, '*The Helsinki Rules, the UN Watercourses Convention and the Berlin Rules: Perspectives on International Water Law*', 23:4 Water Resources Development (2007b): 625–640, at 633.

resolved through negotiation, then the parties shall use other means like fact finding and arbitration (Article 33).

The UN Watercourses Convention reflects core principles of international water law and its provisions have been regarded as customary international law. They have been considered in state practice and by international courts and tribunals in the settlement of international disputes over international watercourses.[131] This UN Convention indeed had a landmark effect in regard to the development of international watercourses law. Commenting on the relevance of this convention, Salman points out that "[s]hared water resources are no longer the only major area without a treaty regulating their uses, sharing, management and protection. For the first time in history, international watercourses are now regulated by a global *framework* Convention that aims at promoting their optimal and sustainable utilization for present and future generations."[132] While there are other instruments that have been updated, for example, the ILA revision of the Helsinki Rules with the 2004 Berlin Rules on Water Resources, they do not have the same status as the UN Watercourses Convention in that they are not binding.[133]

3.1.2 The 1992 UNECE Water Convention and Later Developments

Two major developments can be said to have derived from the work of the UNECE that concern international water law. The first is the Convention on Access to Information, Public Participation in Decision-Making and Access to Justice in Environmental Matters, originally adopted in 1998, which entered

131 Salman 2014, *supra* note 4; Salman 2007b, *id.*; S. C. McCaffrey and M. Sinjela, '*The 1997 United Nations Convention on International Watercourses*', 92:1 The American Journal of International Law (1998): 97–107; *see also* Part 5 of this monograph.

132 Salman 2014, *supra* note 4, at 11–12.

133 The Berlin Rules remark on the obligation to manage the shared watercourse in an equitable and reasonable manner. The 2001 Draft Articles on Prevention of Transboundary Harm noted that the consideration of different factors involves an equitable balance of the states' interests. The Berlin Rules also mention a balancing process between the equitable and reasonable use principle and that of no harm to be worked out in each case individually. *See* ILA, *Report of the 71st Conference* (Berlin, 21 August 2004), at 362 cited in Salman 2007b, *supra* note 130, at 637; ILC, Draft Articles on Prevention of Transboundary Harm from Hazardous Activities, in *Report of the International Law Commission on the work of its fifty-third session (23 April–1 June and 2 July–10 August 2001)*, UN Doc. A/56/10, extract from the Yearbook of the International Law Commission, 2001, Vol. II, Part Two (2001 Draft Articles), art. 10, Commentary (2). In regard to international cooperation and administration of international watercourses, the Berlin Rules do not depart from the Helsinki Rules or the UN Watercourses Convention. As the preceding legal instruments, they establish the basis for the provisions on exchange of information, notification of planned projects or activities, and consultation. Berlin Rules, *id.*, arts. 56, 57, and 58.

into force in 2001.[134] The provisions in this convention highlight the duties of states in the provision of information to prevent environmental damage. The provisions of the Convention have been cited by domestic courts in regional litigation concerning environmental matters.[135]

The second important development concerning water law is the adoption of the Convention on the Protection and Use of Transboundary Watercourses and International Lakes in 1992.[136] The 1992 UNECE Water Convention was initially developed as a regional agreement, but in 2003 the provisions of the Convention restricting it to the regional members were amended. This amendment entered into force in 2013, and since then it allows any other state members of the United Nations to become a contracting party to the Convention.[137]

For the non-navigational uses of watercourses, this effectively means that there are currently two main UN conventions on shared watercourses, the UN Watercourses Convention and the UNECE Water Convention. However, "the UN Watercourse Convention was adopted as a global instrument for the regulation and management of shared watercourses (for non- navigational uses)"[138] from the start, while the UNECE Water Convention started as a regional instrument. Odili summarizes the differences and characteristics between the substantive and procedural rules of the two legal instruments, and though they complement each other, there are some crucial differences, for instance, in the lack of definition of criteria to be taken into account for determining equitable uses, or the lack of detail for the settlement of international disputes in the UNECE Water Convention.[139] The advantages of both instruments, however, is that they can be considered as frameworks to complement independent state practices with regard to shared international watercourses.

134 Convention on Access to Information, Public Participation in Decision-Making and Access to Justice in Environmental Matters, 25 June 1998 (entered into force 30 October 2001).

135 *See* H. Van Loon, '*Global Horizon of Private International Law*', 380 Recueil des Cours (2016): 9–108.

136 The Water Convention, *supra* note 117, was adopted by the senior advisers to the UNECE at their resumed fifth session held at Helsinki from 17 to 18 March 1992.

137 United Nations Economic and Social Council, 'Amendment to Articles 25 and 26 of the Convention,' UN Doc. ECE/MP.WAT/14 (12 January 2004) (Entered into force 6 February 2013).

138 N. C. Odili, '*Shared Water Resources in West Africa*', 3:1 Brill Research Perspectives in International Water Law (2018): 1–98, at 27.

139 *See id.*

3.1.3 Regional South American Developments Concerning the Cuenca del Plata Basin

The 1969 Cuenca del Plata Treaty includes provisions concerning navigation and transport on rivers. Pursuant to these provisions, the cooperation and benefit sharing system of the Plata River Basin was later made more specific. In 1992, the five river basin states established the 'Hydro-way Agreement', which deals solely with navigation through the Parana and Paraguay Rivers.[140] In the same year, the five river basin countries agreed to establish the Hydro-way Intergovernmental Committee (CIH). The CIH Statute mentions its independent legal capacity, but only with regard to hydro-way (navigation) purposes.[141] In 2018, the five river basin countries signed an agreement under which the Hydro-way Agreement's duration was indefinitely extended.[142]

These developments, however, refer to the navigational uses of the rivers. In regards to non-navigation uses, with the exception of administrative issues like appointment of personnel, there have not been any significant developments or new agreements deriving from the Cuenca del Plata Treaty since the Declaration of Asunción of 1971 that would affect or change the countries' position on international rivers.

However, an important new regional treaty concerning aquifers, not international watercourses, the Agreement on the Guarani Aquifer, was signed between Argentina, Brazil, Paraguay, and Uruguay on 2 August 2010. The Guarani aquifer is part of La Plata Basin and the largest sweet (fresh) water reservoir in the world. The agreement entered into force with the ratification of Paraguay in April 2018.[143] It declares the sovereign right of the four countries over the aquifer and establishes a management commitment assuring that its uses shall be reasonable, equitable, and in a sustainable manner. These commitments shall be done by respecting the obligation to not cause any harm to other parties or the environment.[144]

140 Acuerdo de Transporte Fluvial por la Hidrovía Parana-Paraguay (Puerto de Caceres -Puerto de Nueva Palmira), 26 June 1992 (entered into force 13 February 1995); Foreign Affairs Ministers Meeting, Resolution No. 238 (XIX), 26 June 1992, incorporates the Program Hidrovía Parana-Paraguay (Puerto de Caceres-Puerto de Nueva Palmira) into the System of the Cuenca del Plata Treaty.

141 Resolution No. 244 (XX), 5 December 1992, approved in the 20th Reunion of Foreign Affairs Ministers of the La Plata River Basin.

142 8th Additional Protocol to the Hydro-way Agreement, 9 March 2018.

143 Acuerdo Acuífero Guarani (Agreement on the Guarani Aquifer), 2 August 2010. Ratified last by Paraguay under Law 6037/2018 (10 April 2018); Brazil's senate approved it on 2 May 2017; Argentina ratified it under Law 27680 (19 November 2012); and Uruguay ratified it under Senators' chambers File no.72912011 in 2012.

144 Agreement on the Guarani Aquifer, *id.*, art. 3.

3.2 *Advances in International Environmental Law and Climate Change Law*

Further to the legal developments concerning international watercourses, other areas of the law started developing quite rapidly, namely, international environmental law and climate change law, and both are concerned with environmental protection. Since 1970, there have also been important developments with regard to natural resources more generally. In 1974, the United Nations General Assembly adopted the Charter of Economics Rights and Duties.[145] It states that every state shall freely exercise full permanent sovereignty over its wealth, natural resources, and economic activities. In regard to exploitation of natural resources shared by two or more countries, the Charter provides that states "must co-operate on the basis of a system of information and prior consultations in order to achieve optimum use of such resources without causing damage to the legitimate interest of others."[146] In the same year, the UNGA adopted the Declaration on the Establishment of a New International Economic Order, which reinforced rights regarding permanent sovereignty over natural resources.[147] The International Court of Justice (ICJ) further recognized the customary law status of this principle in its judgment in Armed Activities on the Territory of Congo (2005).

International environmental law also embraced the principle and provided a balance between the exercise of state sovereignty and protection of the environment. In 1972, the UN General Assembly supported an international conference which was held in Stockholm from 5 to 16 June 1972. The 114 state participants adopted a set of principles in the Declaration of the UN Conference on the Human Environment (Stockholm Declaration).[148] Of particular relevance here is the original principle 20, which concerned the duty to *inform* other states about activities that might cause significant transboundary environmental harm.[149] However, this original principle 20 on

145 GA Res 3281, UN GAOR, 29th Sess, Supp No. 31, vol. 1, at 50 UN Doc. A/RES/3281 (XXIX 1974), 'Charter of Economic Rights and Duties of States'.

146 *Id.*, art. 3.

147 GA, 3201 (S-VI): Declaration on the Establishment of a New International Economic Order, UN Doc. A/RES/S-6/3201 (1 May 1974).

148 The original declaration of principles prepared by the working group had 23 principles, but some of these principles were contested. It ended up with 26 principles. *See* GA, Report of the United Nations Conference on the Human Environment, Stockholm, 5–16 June 1972, UN Doc. A/CONF.48/14/Rev. 1 (1973).

149 The original principle 20 drafted by the Working Group stated: "Relevant information must be supplied by States on activities or developments within their jurisdiction or under their control whenever they believe, or have reason to believe, that such information is

notification was removed and referred to the UN General Assembly. In this regard, Lammers specifically mentions that one of the factors that caused a lack of consensus for the original principle 20 was the dispute between Argentina and Brazil.[150] Indeed, in relation to the removal of this principle, Angstman et al. commented:

> Argentina wanted to use this principle to deter Brazil from harming its water supply and wildlife by building more and larger dams on the upper Parana river. Brazil mustered more support in the Working Group and the principle was deleted from the Final Declaration.[151]

The notification and consultation points removed from the Stockholm Declaration were sent to the UN General Assembly. By UNGA Resolution 2994, the principles of the Stockholm Conference (without the original principle 20) were accepted. The following UNGA Resolution 2995, as mentioned above, proposed by Brazil and supported by Paraguay, emphasized sovereignty over the exploitation of natural resources and stated that notifications were for purpose of avoiding significant harm, but only in the environment of the adjacent area and that action should not delay nor impede any projects.[152]

Another important principle of the 1972 Stockholm Declaration was Principle 21, which reads:

> States have, in accordance with the Charter of the United Nations and the principles of international law, the sovereign right to exploit their own resources pursuant to their own environmental policies, and the responsibility to ensure that activities within their jurisdiction or control do not cause damage to the environment of other States or of areas beyond the limits of national jurisdiction.[153]

---

needed to avoid the risk of significant adverse effects on the environment in areas beyond their national jurisdiction". *Id.*, Part III: Proceedings of the Conference, para. 331 at 66.

150 J. Lammers, *Pollution of International Watercourses* (Martinus Nijhoff, 1984), at 295.

151 B. L. Angstman, et al.,'*The Stockholm Conference: A Synopsis and Analysis*', 8 Stanford Journal of International Studies (1973): 31, at 42.

152 See Section 2.2.2 above.

153 GA Res 2994, UN GAOR, 27th Sess., Supp. No. 30, at 42, UN Doc. A/RES/2994 (XXVII 1972), United Nations Conference on the Human Environment.

This was reinforced by UNGA Resolution 2996, which stated that no other UN resolution could affect the Principle 21 of the Conference on the Human Environment.[154]

Also in 1972, the United Nations Environment Programme (UNEP) was established to promote international cooperation on environmental issues. In 1973, another UNGA resolution specifically addressed the need for notification and consultation as forms of cooperation in the exploitation of shared natural resources.[155] This resolution was proposed by Argentina, after it had denounced the earlier UNGA Resolution 2995. Both Brazil and Paraguay objected to the 1973 resolution. The principle of notification and consultation was mentioned again the following year in UNGA Resolution 3181, Charter of Economic Rights and Duties, which Brazil rejected.[156]

In 1978, the Governing Council of UNEP adopted the Principles of Conduct in the Field of the Environment for the Guidance of States in the Conservation and Harmonious Utilization of Natural Resources Shared by Two or More States.[157] Principle 6 declares that every state sharing a natural resource with one or more states must notify in advance the other state or states of plans to initiate or change the utilization of the resource which can reasonably be expected to affect significantly the environment in the territory of the other state; enter into consultations concerning the plans; and if there has been no advance notification, "to enter into consultation about plans upon request of the other state."[158] In this regard, exchange of information, notification, and consultation are established as forms of cooperation regarding shared natural resources.

As regards the transition to climate change law affecting water law, it should be noted that the Helsinki Rules in 1966 already mentioned the effect of the climate with regard to the water basin. In 1979 the World Meteorological Organization (WMO) organized the World Climate Conference, which included remarks on the relevance of the climate.[159] The WMO and UNEP proposed

154 GA Res 2996, UN GAOR, 27th Sess., Supp. No. 30, at 42, UN Doc. A/RES/2996 (XXVII 1972), International responsibility of States in regard to the environment.

155 GA Res 3129 (XXVIII), 'Co-operation in the field of the environment concerning natural resources shared by two or more states', *supra* note 99.

156 *See* McCaffrey 2007, *supra* note 9.

157 United Nations Environment Programme (UNEP), Governing Council Decision 6/14, 'Principles of Conduct in the field of the Environment for the Guidance of States in the Conservation and Harmonious Utilization of Natural Resources shared by two or more states', Nairobi, 19 May 1978.

158 *Id.*, principle 6.

159 Proceedings of the World Climate Conference 'A Conference of Experts on Climate and Mankind' Geneva 12–23 February 1979. WMO No. 537; *See* also D. Freestone, '*The*

the establishment of the Intergovernmental Panel on Climate Change (IPCC), which was endorsed by the UN General Assembly in 1988.[160] Freestone describes how in 1990 while preparing for the UN Conference on Environment and Development, there was an agreement that this conference should incorporate an Intergovernmental Negotiating Committee to draft an effective framework convention on climate change.[161] These developments are addressed in greater detail below.

3.2.1 Rio Declaration and UNFCCC

The UN Conference on Environment and Development was held in Rio de Janeiro in 1992. It produced several important documents: the Rio Declaration, the Convention on Biological Diversity, the UN Convention to Combat Desertification, and the UN Framework Convention on Climate Change (UNFCCC). These conventions, though more connected to the protection of the environment and addressing the climate change, are relevant for the non-navigational uses of international watercourses.

The 1992 Rio Declaration copied verbatim Principle 21 of the 1972 Stockholm Declaration, with the additional reference to both "environmental and developmental policies,"[162] and it further states that "the right to development must be fulfilled so as to equitably meet developmental and environmental needs of present and future generations."[163] In regard to notification and consultation, it declares that "States shall provide prior and timely *notification* and relevant information to potentially affected states on activities that may have a significant adverse transboundary environmental effect and shall *consult* with those States at an early stage and in good faith."[164] This phrasing is similar to the excluded original principle 20 of the Stockholm Declaration that was so controversial for Brazil and Argentina, but two decades later, it was accepted by both countries.

United Nations Framework Convention on Climate Change. The Basis for the Climate Change Regime', in C. P. Carlarne, K. Gray & R. Tarasofsky (eds.), *The Oxford Handbook of International Climate Change Law* (Oxford University Press, 2016).

160 GA Res 43/53, UN GAOR, 43rd Sess., Supp. No. 49, vol. 1, at 133, UN Doc. A/43/53 (6 December 1988), 'Protection of global climate for present and future generations of mankind'.

161 Freestone 2016, *supra* note 159.

162 United Nations Conference on Environment and Development, Rio Declaration on Environment and Development, 3–14 June 1992, UN Doc. A/CONF.151/26 (Vol. I) (12 August 1992), Annex I, Principle 2.

163 *Id.*, Principle 3.

164 *Id.*, Principle 19. Emphasis added.

The UNFCCC entered into force in 1994. The non-navigational uses of international rivers such as hydropower production are directly connected to addressing the greenhouse effect. The greenhouse effect would be mitigated by utilization of hydropower, the economic potential derived from one of the common uses of international watercourses. The UNFCCC has adopted a precautionary approach and seeks to the "stabilization of greenhouse gas concentrations in the atmosphere at a level that would prevent dangerous anthropogenic interference with the climate system."[165] Mitigation and adaptation are recommended actions that are supported by the principles stated in Article 3: sustainable development, intergenerational equity, and the principle of common but differentiated responsibility. The UNFCCC also provides financial mechanisms that countries can use to reduce emissions.

The UNFCCC establishes the conference of the parties (COP) as the 'supreme body' of the Convention.[166] It has a permanent secretariat and two subsidiary bodies. The Convention sets out two categories of countries: Annex I, developed countries and economies in transition and Annex II, developing countries.

An important feature of the UNFCCC is its provisions concerning financial resources. The Convention establishes that the developed country parties and other developed parties listed in Annex II

> shall provide new and additional financial resources to meet the agreed full costs incurred by developing country Parties in complying with their obligations under Article 12, paragraph 1[Communication related to implementation]. They shall also provide such financial resources, including for the transfer of technology, needed by the developing country Parties to meet the agreed full incremental costs of implementing measures that are covered by [Article 4, paragraph 1] and that are agreed between a developing countries Party and the international entity or entities referred to in Article 11[financial mechanism], in accordance with that Article.[167]

Further, developed countries are to assist developing country parties in meeting the costs of adaptation to those adverse effects (Article 4 (4)), transfer technology and know-how (Article 4(5)), and assist them in meeting their communication obligations under Article 12 and in implementing measures for

165 United Nations Framework Convention on Climate Change (UNFCCC), 9 May 1992 (entered into force 21 March 1994), art. 2.

166 *Id.*, art. 7(4).

167 *Id.*, art. 4(3).

the fulfilment of their commitments (Article 4(1)). The Global Environmental Facility was established to manage the financial mechanism.[168]

3.2.2 The Kyoto Protocol

At the first UNFCCC COP meeting in 1995, and through a mandate to work on the adequacy of the requirements of Article 4 (to return anthropogenic GHG emission to 1990 levels), the decision was taken to strengthen the commitment in Article 4 for Annex I countries through the adoption of a protocol. This led to the adoption of the 1997 Kyoto Protocol.[169]

The 1997 Kyoto Protocol has an innovative trading mechanism to help the parties achieve their emission reduction objectives. Freestone identifies three components and summarizes their provisions as follows:

> 1) Joint Implementation: Annex I countries finance a project in a host country. "The host country agrees that GHG emission reductions generated by that project will be transferred as Emission Reduction Units (ERUs) to the financing country or countries ... Reductions of GHGs in one country are financed by another which can then claim the credit againstitscap."[170]
>
> 2) Clean Development Mechanism: "Financed from penalties paid by Annex I countries for non-compliance with emission reduction targets that would in turn finance low-carbon 'clean' development projects in developing countries.... Annex I countries with Kyoto emission reduction (ER) commitments finance projects in developing countries (non-Annex I countries, which have no Kyoto ER commitments) that promote sustainable development and also reduce GHG emissions. The Annex I countries can then claim credit against their own Kyoto targets for the emissions reductions that an independent party can certify would not have taken place in the host country without their financing. Hence these projectsgeneratewhatarecalledCertifiedEmissionReductions(CERs)."[171]

---

168 *Id.*, art. 21(3).

169 D. Freestone *'The International Climate Change Legal and Institutional Framework: An Overview'*, in D. Freestone & C. Streck (eds.), *Legal Aspects of Carbon Trading* (Oxford University Press, 2009); Freestone 2016, *supra* note 159.

170 D. Freestone *'The International Climate Change Legal and Institutional Framework: An Overview'* in David Freestone, Charlotte Streck (eds) *Legal Aspects of Caron Trading* (Oxford University Press 2009); Freestone 2016, *id.*, at 13.

171 Freestone 2009, *id.*; Freestone 2016, *id.*, at 14.

In this regard the COP set up an executive board to supervise the Clean Development Mechanism. The financing of this board comes from a share of proceeds of the projects, which are put in an Adaptation Fund.

3) Emission Trading or Assigned Amount Trading: Although everyone can trade emission rights, transfers are only affected by parties of the Protocol.[172]

3.2.3 The 2015 Paris Agreement

To enhance the implementation of the UNFCCC, the COP adopted the 2015 Paris Agreement which sets out the objectives to hold the increase in the global average temperature to below 2 degrees Celsius, increase the ability of states to adapt to adverse impacts of climate change, and to make financial flows consistent with the aim of reducing emissions. The Paris Agreement set outs the commitment of the parties and calls on them to communicate their contributions to reducing the emissions through their own domestic policies, which is known as the Intended Nationally Determined Contributions. Although the parties have the opportunity to change and adapt this communication, climate change litigation has shown how states can be bound to these international commitments.[173] The international community faced a disappointment with the decision of the United States to pull out of the Paris Agreement, but as of January 2019 the Agreement has 197 signatories and has been ratified by 184 countries, which reflects the wide acceptance of its provisions.

3.2.4 The 2001 ILC Articles on Prevention of Transboundary Harm

The ILC adopted the Draft Articles on Prevention of Transboundary Harm from Hazardous Activities in 2001.[174] The Draft Articles establish the requirement that a state "shall take all appropriate measures to prevent significant transboundary harm or at any event to minimize the risk thereof."[175] Such measures include an assessment, as well as the environmental assessment. In this regard, the Draft Articles call for notification and consultation to minimize risk.

The Draft Articles also provide that there should be an 'equitable balance of interests.' This implies that states must take into account different factors when engaging in transboundary activities. Indeed, the Draft Articles list factors, such as the degree of risk of harm and the availability of means to prevent

172 These provisions were set in the COP meeting in Marrakech in 2001. *See* Freestone 2016, *id.*, at 15.

173 *Stichting Urgenda v The State of the Netherlands*, The Hague District Court, 24 June 2015, ECLI:NL:RBDHA:2015:7196.

174 2001 Draft Articles, *supra* note 133.

175 *Id.*, art. 3.

or minimize harm; the importance of the activity taking into account its overall advantages of a social, economic and technical character for the state of origin in relation to the potential harm to another state; harm to the environment; the degree to which the state of origin and, as appropriate, the state likely to be affected are prepared to contribute to the costs of prevention of harm; economic viability of the activity; standards of prevention which the state likely to be affected applies to the same or comparable activities; and the standards applied in comparable regional or international practice.[176] The commentaries discussing these factors expressly refer to the precautionary principle, which states "environmental measures must anticipate, prevent and attack the causes of environmental degradation. Where there are threats of serious or irreversible damage, lack of full scientific certainty should not be used as a reason for postponing measures to prevent environmental degradation."[177]

Now having had an overview of some of the key developments and advancements in international water law and international environmental and climate change law, we now turn to the implementation of the 1973 treaty for the uses of the Parana River to obtain hydropower, the Itaipu Treaty. These developments in environmental and climate change law form an important backdrop to its implementation. They have been largely ignored in the implementation of the Itaipu Treaty thus far, but will arguably play a crucial role in the renegotiation of the Treaty in 2023.

Part 4: Implementation of the Itaipu Treaty and the Energy Policy Paradox in Paraguay: a Case for Updating the Treaty?

In order to see the advantages of adapting a bilateral treaty to current international law developments, as proposed by the UN Watercourses Convention, we must look first at how a treaty has been implemented without taking heed of the development of international law over the last 40 years, and then discuss how things could be changed for the better by taking these developments into account. The Itaipu Treaty is a perfect example for this. First, we shall look at how it has been implemented over the last half century and how it has affected the countries' domestic energy policies. Only Paraguay does not use its entire share of the energy produced by the dam, so the focus will be on Paraguay's

176 *Id.*, art. 10.

177 Action for a Common Future: Report of the Economic Commission for Europe on the Bergen Conference, 8–16 May 1990, UN ECE Doc. A/CONF.151/PC/10 Annex I, para. 7; Draft Articles, *id.*, art. 10(6), commentary.

domestic energy policies. It is also the country that faces an energy policy paradox, as will be explained below.

The Itaipu project, through the building of a dam in the international Parana River, can be considered successful because of the sheer amount of renewable energy it has produced. The Itaipu entity has produced 2,494,083 GWh since it was created, or 11,769,2199 MWA of clean renewable energy per year, which amounts to the world's highest production of renewable energy.[178]

When looking at the effects on the environment, and comparing this renewable energy to the effect that other sources of energy would have on the environment, there are strong arguments for the use of renewable energy. For instance, if this amount of energy were to be produced by non-renewable sources of energy, it would produce carbon dioxide emission of 41 million tonnes (from gas-fired plants); 72 million tonnes (from oil-fired plants); or 93 million tonnes (from coal-fired plants).[179]

Brazil and Paraguay own equal shares of the energy produced by Itaipu.[180] Thus, for Paraguay, this amounts to 5,884,5 MWA per year. Paraguay's total demand of energy, which is currently the highest in its history, is 3,097 MWA per year,[181] which is half of what they effectively own (Table 1).

Paraguay does not use much of its share of Itaipu energy to satisfy its energy demand; instead, Paraguay centers its consumption on energy produced from biomass and oil. According to the Paraguayan Sub-Secretary of Energy, 44.2 percent of the energy Paraguay actually uses comes from biomass, 40.1 percent from oil, and only 15.7 percent from hydroelectricity.[182] The usage of Paraguay's

178 This corresponds to production in 2016. 'Energy', Itaipu Binacional, https://www.itaipu.gov.br/en/energy/energy (last accessed 14 February 2019). The generation value decreased in 2018.

179 *Id.*

180 Shareholders of the Itaipu entity created by the Treaty are the national electricity companies of the respective countries: Eletrobras (Brazil) and Asociación Nacional de Electricidad ANDE (Paraguay). Both companies wholly owned or controlled by the respective countries.

181 This was reported to be the energy demand in 2017. ANDE, '*El Sector Electrico Paraguayo: Evolucion y Desafios de la ANDE*', Presentation, 26 May 2017.

182 Viceministerio de Minas y Energía (Paraguay). Balance Energético Nacional 2017, August 2018, at 26. https://www.ssme.gov.py/vmme/pdf/balance2017/BEN2017.pdf (Last accessed 14 February 2019). *See* also Viceministerio de Minas y Energía (Paraguay) Resena Energética — Consumo Final de Energía. Sistema de Información Energética Nacional (SIEN) de la Dirección de Recursos Energéticos Primarios del Vice Ministerio de Minas y Energía.
https://www.ssme.gov.py/vmme/index.php?option=com_content&view=article&id=1213&Itemid=598 (Last accessed 14 February 2019).

TABLE 1 Paraguay's share of the Itaipu energy and effective use (MWA)

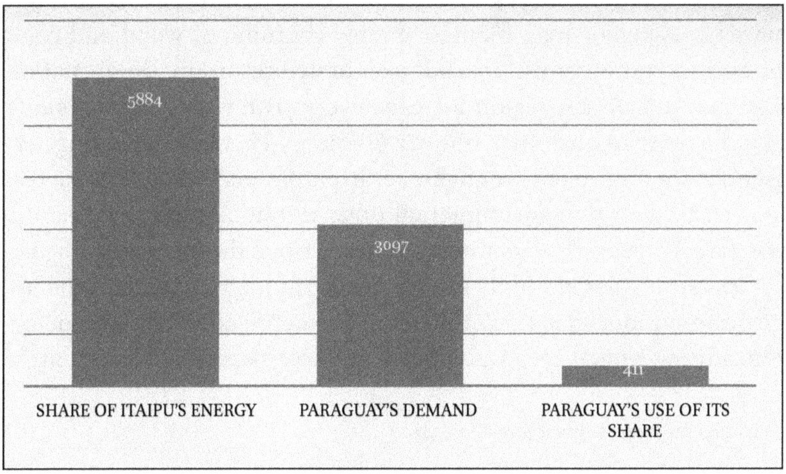

SOURCE: TABLE BASED ON THE INFORMATION PROVIDED BY THE ASOCIACIÓN NACIONAL DE ELECTRICIDAD (ANDE), 'EL SECTOR ELECTRICO PARAGUAYO: EVOLUCION Y DESAFIOS DE LA ANDE', PRESENTATION, 26 MAY 2017.

TABLE 2 Sources of energy consumption in Paraguay

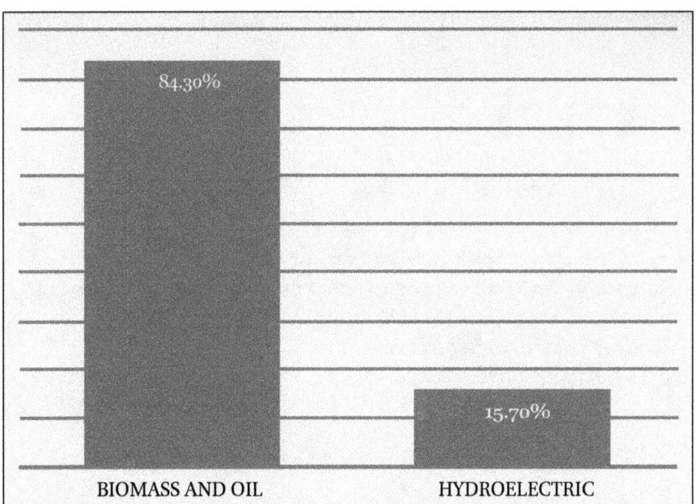

SOURCE: TABLE BASED ON THE INFORMATION PROVIDED BY THE PARAGUAYAN SUB-SECRETARY OF ENERGY AND MINES, OFFICIAL ANNUAL REPORT, YEAR 2017.

50 percent share of hydroelectric energy from the Itaipu dam has varied, some years it has been 15 percent, but lately it is reported to be only 7 percent.[183]

Paraguay's heavy reliance on biomass energy (burning of wood and coal) results not only in carbon emissions, but also in deforestation. Deforestation rates in Paraguay and in the region increase every year, with Paraguay's rate increasing at faster than any other country (Table 3). This has substantial adverse consequences for the environment. For example, according to the latest study of a forest watch non-governmental organization, Paraguay is leading the charts in terms of loss of intact forests. This is despite the fact that Paraguay could easily cover 100 percent of its energy needs through its share of the hydroelectric power produced at the Itaipu dam. The connection between deforestation and adverse effects on a water basin are well-established by scientific

TABLE 3 Global ranking of intact forest loss (IFL)

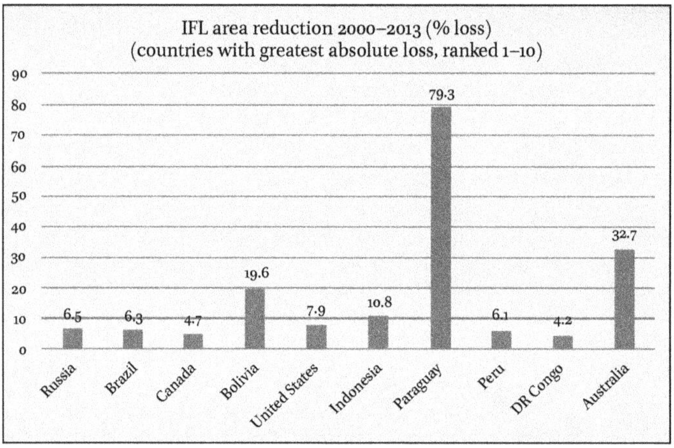

SOURCE: DATA FROM POTAPOV ET AL., '*THE LAST FRONTIERS OF WILDERNESS: TRACKING LOSS OF INTACT FOREST LANDSCAPES FROM 2000 TO 2013*' 3:1 SCIENCE ADVANCES E1600821(2017), TABLE 2; CANNON,J. MONGABAY SERIES: GLOBAL FOREST REPORTING NETWORK (13 JANUARY 2017).

183 Itaipu Binacional, '*Prestación de los Servicios de Electricidad y Bases Financieras: Compendio*' (Grafica Asuncena, 2003) (hereinafter Itaipu Binacional 2003); 'Paraguay recibe solo el 7% de la energía producida por Itaipú', *ABC Color* (Paraguay) (17 March 2017). In August 2017, this percentage increased according to the Itaipu entity, but the Sub-Secretary of Energy reported that it had actually decreased. The remaining difference in hydropower that is used comes from other hydropower dams that Paraguay has.

and technical studies.[184] Further, such energy generation policies go against crucial international legal principles and obligations, such as protecting and preserving the ecosystem of watercourses, or reducing emissions.

Given that Paraguay is one of the biggest hydroelectric power producers per capita in the world, it is paradoxical that it does not take advantage of this potential and relies instead on biomass energy and oil (which it imports) for most of its domestic energy consumption, covering only a small percentage through hydroelectric energy (which it fully owns). Though many uses, for example, farming, may have deforestation consequences, the Itaipu Treaty has had a significant impact on the adoption of these Paraguayan domestic policies, as will be discussed below.

The Itaipu Treaty regulates every aspect of the use of the river to produce hydropower, as well as the management, service, and consumption of this energy.[185] In Paraguay, the Itaipu Treaty has played a key role in domestic policies. During the 1980s, the Paraguayan Congress debated which energy policies should be followed and implemented. The Congress debated what they called the agro-export surplus model on the one hand, and the import-substituting industrialization model on the other. In spite of being domestic energy policies, these debates have taken into account the Itaipu Treaty and the Itaipu entity given that Itaipu energy is the main source and generator of energy. However, Itaipu is a binational endeavor, and so the administrative structure of the Itaipu entity, which is shared by Paraguay and Brazil, has had a substantial influence in domestic energy policy.[186]

The agro-export surplus model is based on selling excess energy to Brazil and using that revenue to develop Paraguay's agricultural industry. Paraguay uses Brazilian machinery and expertise, and it is therefore not surprising that the agro-export surplus model was always favored by Brazil.[187]

The alternative import-substitute model would mean increasing Paraguay's consumption of its hydroelectric energy share and using this energy to industrialize. Among the advocates of this model was the Paraguayan Industrial

184 Y. Malhi, et al.,'*Climate Change, Deforestation, and the Fate of the Amazon*', 319:5860 Science (2008):169–172; P. Potapov, et al., '*The Last Frontiers of Wilderness: Tracking Loss of Intact Forest Landscapes from 2000 to 2013*', 3:1 Science Advances e1600821(2017); L. Saenz '*Assessing Impacts of Deforestation in Itaipu's Dam Watershed in Paraguay*' (World Resources Institute, July 2018).

185 Paraguay's National Constitution establishes a hierarchy in the legal order; following the national constitution, treaties take precedence over national laws.

186 See further Section 4.1.3. in this monograph.

187 See Soares de Lima, *supra* note 63, for details.

Union. Since the 1980s the Paraguayan Industrial Union has pointed out that the energy policy of the country should not be the 'export of surplus' model. They argue that the energy policy should favor increased use of Paraguay's energy quota to stimulate domestic industrialization. The main criticism of this approach in the 1980s was that to develop the use of this energy, Paraguay would have to incur international debt and seek foreign investors willing to participate in the industrialization process.[188]

However, despite choosing the export of surplus model, Paraguay did not avoid debt, as will be described shortly, and it has not really industrialized either.[189] Paraguay has the potential to attract foreign investments because it has one of the best international investment frameworks in the region, providing guarantees to foreign investors through its National Constitution and an array of bilateral investment treaties (which most countries in the region have terminated).[190] Despite this, as recently as 2016 Paraguay enacted by decree its new energy policy, which, by not making any express mention of an increase in the use of hydropower, implicitly recommits to the agro-export surplus model, which the country has followed since the 1980s.[191]

188 Also expressed in the views of then President of the ANDE, Mr. Enzo Debernardi, before numerous public entities. E. Debernardi 'Estrategia de Desarrollo en Condiciones de Oferta Abundante de Energía Eléctrica' IDB Minutes of Congress, 28 July–1 August 1980, Asuncion, Paraguay; Debernardi, *supra* note 26, c IX, XIII; *see* also Contraloria General de la Republica, Resolution No.346 17 April 1997; Nickson, *supra* note 50.

189 According to the 2013 Electricity Program in Brazil, Brazil provided electricity to 14.8 million habitants, at no charge for electric connection and with discounts on the price of electricity. In Paraguay, with a population that does not exceed 6.8 habitants, there have been increases in the price of electricity, and there is no budget to improve the infrastructure and there are regular blackouts throughout the year. See International Energy Agency, *World Energy Outlook 2013* (IEA, 12 November 2013).

190 Paraguayan National Constitution, arts. 88, 107, and 109; Foreign Investment Law No. 117/91 provides the same guarantees, rights, and obligations enjoyed by Paraguayan investors. For a list of bilateral investment treaties (BITs) ratified by Paraguay see UNCTAD Investment Policy Hub database, https://investmentpolicyhub.unctad.org/IIA.

191 Decree No. 6092, 10 October 2016, approves the Energy Policy of Paraguay which is detailed in an annex. Although it shows some improvement as to having clear guidelines in this area, its objectives, *inter alia*, refer to the use of the hydropower, but rather than suggesting an increase of its use, the policy states that use and production of hydrocarbons to produce energy should be intensified. It also provides for continued use and promotion of bioenergy, which includes biomass. See Decree, Table 1, s. 1.3.(10) and Annex, Table 9 (7,8). Section 1.5.2 of the Decree relates to hydropower, detailing intended development in the region, but there is no mention of an increase in the use of it.

4.1 *Itaipu Treaty Provisions Affecting Energy Policy in Paraguay*

As a matter of international law and national legislation, it is important to pay attention to the key provisions in the Itaipu Treaty that have a direct impact on Paraguayan domestic energy policies. Since these policies also affect the environment, it is important to analyze the implementation of the Treaty in the light of the protection of the water basin that sources the river that enables the Itaipu dam to produce such large amounts of energy. The following discussion examines provisions that restrict the use of renewable energy and third-party sales, affect the price of energy, and deal with dispute settlement.

4.1.1 Provisions Restricting the Use of Renewable Energy and Third-Party Sale Restrictions

Prior to signing the Itaipu Treaty, fossil fuel energy sources were not sufficient to meet the demands of domestic energy consumption of Brazil. Brazil had the option of developing nuclear energy with German cooperation, but those involved in developing Brazil's energy policies preferred a renewable energy source rather than the nuclear alternative. The Minister of Energy of Brazil, speaking at Brazil's Congress in 1973, stated that Brazil's annual demand for electricity was growing by 12 percent per annum in regions that were already being served; in other regions, the growth was even greater. He argued that Brazil needed to increase its electrical energy production and that Itaipu was the best source to satisfy that demand.[192]

Brazil's strategy to secure the energy it needed was reflected in the subsequent bilateral treaties that it signed with Paraguay. As discussed above, the 1966 Acta de Yguazu, a document preceding the Itaipu Treaty regarding the exploitation of the Parana River, included a paragraph that stated that if the energy produced by the dam exceeded one of the two countries' needs, the excess would have to be offered to the other signatory country before offering it to any third party. The same paragraph, amended by a further restriction, was included in the Itaipu Treaty. The Itaipu Treaty established that the unused energy share that belonged to one party has to be sold 'solely' to the other party (Article XIII). In other words, Paraguay can only sell its unused share of energy to Brazil. As we can see from these terms of the Treaty, as well as of the favored approach toward the agro-export surplus model described above, it was never in Brazil's interest for Paraguay to increase its consumption of energy, because Brazil would then get less energy to meet its own demands.

The Itaipu Treaty also requires each party to present a schedule of the yearly amount of electricity they intended to consume in a ten-year period two years

192 Session at the Deputy Chamber, 24 May 1973, Debernardi, *supra* note 26, at 260.

in advance of the respective decade. The Treaty had initially established that this should be done for 20 years, but this was later reduced to ten years.[193] This remains, however, a massive restriction for the free disposition of energy intended for domestic consumption. It effectively means that no Paraguayan administration can significantly change the energy policy of the country (in particular, decide that Paraguay would use more of its share of hydroelectric energy) during the time it is in power. Moreover, by an exchange of notes between the two governments on the same day that the Treaty was signed, it was established that Brazil, through Eletrobras, would acquire the total amount of power produced by the hydroelectric dam in the first place, and would pass on the Paraguayan share of power based on its ten-year schedule.[194]

Together, the third-party sale restriction and the restriction to fixing consumption indexes for ten years gives Brazil an astoundingly asymmetrical share of power over the day-to-day operations of the plant and long-term planning concerning the use of the energy.

These provisions are very different to how other countries handle similar situations. In other countries, contracting energy is typically governed by power purchase agreements, which are much more short term. In such contracts, the guaranteed amount energy can vary from year to year or even from month to month.[195] This market practice has the advantage of not locking either party in for an extended period of time, and it does not restrict the selling party from considering offers to purchase the energy under better terms. Indeed, other countries in the region have expressed an interest in buying the excess of energy that Paraguay has at a much better price than the one which Brazil pays; but Paraguay is restricted to sell it to another country pursuant to the Treaty, and due to its lack of infrastructure to transport the energy. On this last point how-

193 Itaipu Treaty, *supra* note 101, Annex C, II.2 and II.3. In the Yacyreta Treaty, this provision is for eight years. This restricts the domestic market consumption in advance. *See further* Soares de Lima, *supra* note 63; da Rosa, *supra* note 67.

194 *Nota reversal* between the two governments on the same day of signature of the treaty. Brazil established that through Eletrobras it would acquire the total power of the hydroelectric dam, and the power that is contracted by ANDE would be deducted from this. *See* Nota Reversal No. 5, 26 April 1973.

195 See, for example, power purchase agreements (PPAs). Also see practices around medium term offers in Mexico, which average a three — year term. Funcion Publica, Portal del Gobierno de Mexico, http://www.cenace.gob.mx/SIM/VISTA/REPORTES/SubMedianoPlazo.aspx and 'Gobierno presenta subasta eléctrica de mediano plazo,' *Forbes Mexico* (13 August 2017), https://www.forbes.com.mx/gobierno-presenta-subasta-electrica-de-mediano-plazo/ (last accessed 22 March 2018); see also various models of PPAs in England, in which terms are, for example, just five years in the short term. 'Power Purchase Agreements,' Statkraft UK Ltd., https://www.statkraft.co.uk/power-purchase-agreements/.

ever, and since the lack of infrastructure has also been an obstacle for Paraguay to increase its hydroelectric energy consumption, it is worth noting the other provisions of the Treaty impacting this, namely, the price of energy.

Paraguay lacks the necessary infrastructure because it has a budget deficit; plainly, it does not have enough money in its infrastructure budget to build the necessary infrastructure. Thus it sells a huge part of its hydroelectric energy to Brazil, which does have the necessary infrastructure to distribute the energy to its most populous areas (for the difference in transmission lines capacities see Figure 2). The price of energy is therefore directly connected to this factor.

4.1.2 The Price of Energy under the Itaipu Treaty

The provisions concerning determination the price of energy are found in Annex C of the Itaipu Treaty. The Treaty establishes that the price should be equal to the cost of energy. The energy is acquired by the two national electricity entities respectively. In practice, however, Eletrobras acquires the whole power produced by the dam and ANDE receives its share from them.

Annex C, Chapter III, lists the different items that contribute to the total price of energy that the two national electricity companies pay to the Itaipu entity. Under the original provisions of the Treaty, eight factors were used:

1. Necessary amount for payment of 12 percent return on the capital stock. This percentage is calculated annually, and the provision was set to secure a return to the capital contributed by both countries, which was US$100 million, to establish the binational entity Itaipu.
2. Necessary amount for payment of financial charges from loans.
3. Necessary amount for payment of amortization of the loans. Items 2 and 3 refer to all the loans, as well as repayment of capital and interest that the entity undertook.
4. Necessary amount for payment of royalties: US$650/GWh generated. This is the amount to be paid to the countries because they are the owner of the resource being used (water).
5. Necessary amount for payment to ANDE and Eletrobras for administrative charges, US$50/GWh.
6. Amount necessary to cover exploitation expenses.
7. The difference (positive or negative) of the exploitation expenses from the previous year.
8. Amount for compensation: US$300/GWh. This is the remuneration that has to be given to the country that is not using the energy and is ceded to the other country. In practice, this is the payment for the energy that Paraguay sells to Brazil (Brazil never sells to Paraguay but uses its entire share of energy itself).

TABLE 4 Ratio of debt payment in the price of energy

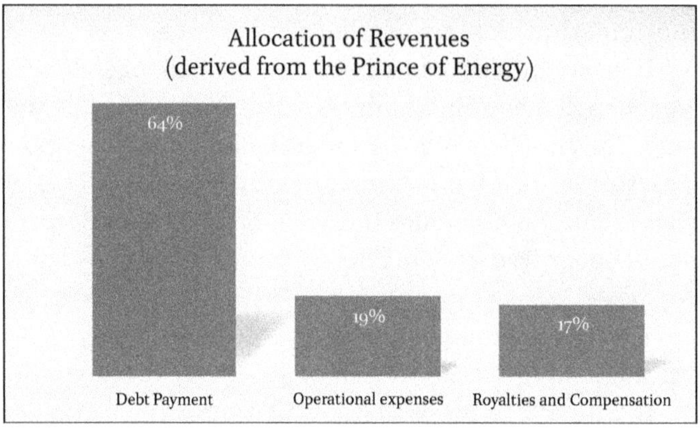

SOURCE: PERCENTAGES MENTIONED IN THE DEBT ANALYSIS IN M. A. ZYDAN SORIA, *USINA DE ITAIPU. INTEGRACAO ENERGÉTICA ENTRE BRASIL E PARAGUAI* (EDITORA UFPR, 2012).

Overall, the items constituting the price could be classified as those regarding debt repayment, those regarding operational expenses, and those regarding royalties and compensation. Table 4 sets out the proportion of revenues allocated to cover these items. As Table 4 shows, the difference in how the revenues are allocated to pay each item (all of which are included in the price of energy) shows the priority of paying back debt.[196]

The compensation item (8) was expressly part of the price of energy in the Treaty until 1986, when it was removed. This removal from the items making up the price of energy was important, as it meant that the country that sells its excess of energy, in practice only Paraguay, would be paying for such a sale as well.[197]

A further modification was made to the price when a regulation was added to Annex C. The regulation was approved by the Administrative Council of the Itaipu entity in 1997. Though this was done without parliamentary approval, it made a substantial modification to the price as it established a tariff. The tariff was determined to be the unit for the sale of the product. The tariff is derived from the annual cost of electricity service divided by the contracted power that the national electricity companies commit to purchase. This was thought to

196 Percentages included in the debt analysis are from Zydan Soria, *supra* note 31. They are derived from the total revenue of Itaipu.

197 It was done through Note No. 4, 28 April 1986.

be a more flexible mechanism as it has had the effect of contracting the price based on the different demands for power of each country.[198]

4.1.2.1 *The Debt*

The debt of the project is expected to be paid off by the established time of renegotiation, that is, 50 years after the conclusion of the Itaipu Treaty, in the year 2023. However, it is important to consider the background to this debt as it has affected the price of energy for half a century.

The creation of Itaipu resulted in two types of debts: the capital required to constitute the binational entity, Itaipu, and the loans to cover the construction of the dam. When the Treaty was signed in 1973, the calculated cost was US$1.8 billion.[199] However, Zydan Soria argues that the total debt accumulated between 1974 and 2011 (the capital to incorporate the entity plus construction costs) reached US$27.1 billion.[200]

Although the Itaipu entity was established to take out the loans, it is important to note that the main creditor of the loans was Eletrobras. Over the years, Eletrobras has remained the main creditor of Itaipu, and later assigned these credits to the Brazilian National Treasury.[201] Other Brazilian entities also provided loans.

Despite this loan history, Brazil never agreed to pay more for the project than Paraguay.[202] The loans are established in separate contracts signed between the creditors and the Itaipu entity; these agreements contain provisions regarding interest rates, terms, etc. However, the loans are also directly linked to the Itaipu Treaty because it establishes that the debts would be paid through the price of energy.[203]

---

198 The Itaipu entity created an Annex C Regulation that was approved through a Resolution of the Council of Administration of the entity, RCA-002/97, on 7 March 1997. The Itaipu Treaty, *supra* note 101, establishes that the revenue is equal to the cost of energy (price). The tariff or unitary cost of energy is applied by having the cost divided by contracted power.

199 da Rosa, *supra* note 67.

200 *See* Zydan Soria, *supra* note 31, at 128.

201 *Id.*

202 The history of this loan includes the government of Paraguay objecting to being a guarantor of any debt regarding the Itaipu project due to difficulties with the economic realities of Paraguay. This view was expressed in various Paraguayan Congressional sessions. Since the creditor is an entity controlled by the Brazilian state, and the debt was assigned to the Brazilian Treasury, the financial flows, including calculated interest, goes directly back to Brazil.

203 Itaipu Treaty, *supra* note 101, Annex C, III.3.

The amount of debt increased was a consequence of the default on payments of the initial debt. This situation can be explained by the international financial situation in the late 1970s.[204] The Itaipu entity indicated that, at the time, there was no way to refinance these loans in a way that would be flexible enough to allow construction to proceed, especially considering that the necessary financing needs were very high. It has been argued that this is why the Brazilian loans were the only way to increase the availability of credit for Itaipu.[205]

There were other options, for instance obtaining international financing, but Brazil argued against these alternatives.[206] Brazil objected to obtaining international financing to cover the increased costs based on the argument that financing from international institutions would require agreeing to conditions such as international procurement for provision of equipment and services, and pursuant to the Treaty both countries, Brazil and Paraguay, intended to build the dam with local labor, equipment, and products.[207] The Itaipu Treaty stated "the labour … the equipment and the materials, available in the two countries, shall be utilized in an equitable manner."[208] However, some of the loans taken from Brazilian entities also included conditions to use solely Brazilian labor and products.[209] As a result, out of the companies that participated in building the dam, only 15 percent were Paraguayan companies, with the remainder being Brazilian. Further, most of the products and labor used were Brazilian.[210]

The increased debt also resulted from the fact that Itaipu was providing energy to Eletrobras, which in turn provided the energy to other Brazilian energy companies. Due to Brazil's internal economic crisis throughout the 1980s and 1990s, which also affected the energy sector, these companies did not pay for the energy, and the lack of payment to Itaipu in turn affected Itaipu's ability to pay its debt. At this stage, the creditor and shareholder of Itaipu, Eletrobras, did not refinance the existing debt; instead it provided more loans to cover the default.[211]

---

204 The international financial flows in the late 1970s affected many developing countries. They were not able to commit to the high interest rates on their foreign debt, which eventually led to the Latin American debt crisis. The latter took place when the Itaipu Dam was being built. Itaipu Binacional 2003, *supra* note 183.

205 *Id.*

206 Debernardi, *supra* note 26.

207 Itaipu Binacional 2003, *supra* note 183, at 75.

208 Itaipu Treaty, *supra* note 101, art. XI, para. 1.

209 These were in loans given by the Special Agency for Industrial Financing (FINAME), a subsidiary of the National Brazilian Development Bank (BNDES).

210 Nickson, *supra* note 50; Soares de Lima, *supra* note 63.

211 Itaipu Binacional 2003, *supra* note 183.

Additionally, the main debt to Eletrobras was in Brazilian currency, cruzeiros, and an internal Brazilian index for market prices was applied. When the currency suffered as a result of inflation, this also affected the debt, which, as a consequence, increased by 40 percent.[212] When Brazil replaced the cruzeiros with a new currency, the real, in 1994, this likewise had consequences for the debt. Itaipu's 2003 compendium describes the increase of debt by US$ 3.7 billion, and the tariff adjustments (some of which were not even applied in 1986 due to Brazil's financial crisis) all contributed to the inability to pay the debt.[213] Only in 1997 did the main creditor, Eletrobras, agree to 'dollarize' the debt and reduce the interest rate of the debt. However, this required the tariff to increase by 7 percent, plus a factor of adjustment that varies every year depending on the respective inflation of the dollar.[214]

By including the debt repayment in the energy price, the Treaty established long-term commitments for Itaipu (and effectively its shareholders) to pay back its debt to Brazil. The interest rate and application of indexes on the debt were tailored to the Brazilian market. The conditions were such that the debt could only be paid fully after half a century. This raises the question of the premise at the time regarding international financing. The parties did not obtain equitable participation in labor. One can consider whether repayment of the debt, if it had been tailored to the international market rather than to Brazil's internal economy, would have been reduced.

It is also important to note that since the application of the tariff in 1997, Brazil, by contracting more power, pays more than Paraguay on the debt. This scheme continues to provide the cheapest energy that Brazil can get in the market, and what Brazil contributes towards the debt all flows back to the Brazilian Treasury.[215] This allows the country to industrialize using this energy, a situation very different to that of Paraguay.

212 *Id.*, at 84.

213 *Id.*, at 87.

214 Exchange of Notes No. 3, 28 January 1986; *see also* Itaipu Binacional 2003, *id.*, at 89.

215 Electrobras is a publicly-held, government controlled company and has assigned its credit to the Brazilian National Treasury. For recent changes in corporate structure *see* its description in Eletrobras, Annual Report 2017. Even more recently, according to the Business and Management Master Plan (PDNG) 2018–2022 Eletrobras informed that the Company's Board of Directors approved the transfer to Eletrobras holding of certain equity interests held by the subsidiaries in special purpose companies (SPE), as well as corporate ventures. The aforementioned operation represented one of the stages of the then 2017/2021 PDNG and are maintained in the PDNG of 2018–2022, disclosed to the market on 17 December 2017. The next step is the sale of these SPEs by Eletrobras. The Brazilian Ministry of Mines and Energy proposed the privatization of Eletrobras but it will depend on legislative authorization. See full details in Eletrobras 'Investor Relations' FAQ http://eletrobras.com/en/ri/Paginas/FAQ.aspx (last accessed 19 February 2019).

4.1.2.2 *Royalties and Compensation*

The Itaipu Treaty has a clause under which the parties agreed to exempt from taxes everything concerning the project, which, though an incentive, provides no revenue to the countries. Considering that all machinery and services used in the dam were mainly from Brazilian sources, this benefited Brazil more than Paraguay.[216] However, revenues, royalties, and compensation are sources of income for both countries. These items, in addition to the debt repayment and other operational costs, were also included as costs to determine the price of energy.

Royalties are the remuneration to Brazil and Paraguay for the use of the river. Independently, the price also contained 'compensation' as an item, which determines what Paraguay gets for selling its unused energy to Brazil. This item was later removed from the price calculation for the reasons described above: including compensation in the general price meant that if Paraguay sold its unused energy to Brazil, it partially paid for that very energy itself when it paid the Itaipu entity for the energy that it did use. Thus, compensation was removed from the items comprising the general price by an exchange of notes in 1986. But since Paraguay is the only country selling excess energy, the established amount for compensation is clearly more relevant for Paraguay.[217]

The Itaipu Treaty fixes the base price of energy for both royalties and compensation.[218] The price that the Treaty establishes differs radically from that of market value. For instance, comparing the total price of Itaipu with another regional hydropower operation, Brazil currently obtains the energy from Itaipu at US$10 per MWh, but it pays Uruguay US$112–136 per MWh for the same kind of energy.[219]

---

216 Itaipu Treaty, *supra* note 101, art. XII.

217 It is important to note that in 1973, the calculation of the base amount of both royalties and compensation did not include factors such as the variation in costs of the project, costs resulting from considering water as an economic rent, or adaptation to changes in market values.

218 Base amount for royalties US$650 GWh; for compensation US$300 GWh. After the Exchange of Notes, 28 January 1986, the formula for both base amounts was changed to differed payment to the year 1992, in which the established base amount would be multiplied by 4 and at factors of adjustment of the year 1986.

219 'Abdicación de la Soberanía en las Usinas Binacionales', *ABC Color* (Paraguay) (21 May 2017). Toledano & Maennling report US$9,350 GWh in compensation for 2012. *See* P. Toledano & N. Maennling '*Leveraging Paraguay's Hydropower for Sustainable Economic Development*', Vale Columbia Center on Sustainable International Investment, November 2013, at 61; 'Venta de Energia a Brasil sumar $36 millones en el año', *El Observador* (Montevideo), 23 September 2017 reports the average price for which Uruguay sells its hydroelectric energy to Brazil is US$79 MWh.

The terms for calculating compensation were modified in 2009. At the insistence of Paraguayan authorities, the compensation that Paraguay gets from the energy sold to Brazil was increased. Paraguay and Brazil reached a settlement by which the compensation was multiplied by a factor of 15.3, instead of a factor of 4 that was applied in 1992.[220] This effectively increased the amount that Paraguay gets for ceding the energy that it does not use to Brazil, as compared to what it was getting for the energy over the last 36 years.[221] There is little information as to why that particular number was agreed upon. Maurer concluded:

> In July 2009, Brazil signed a generous settlement with Paraguay regarding revenues from the Itaipu Dam, shared between the two countries. The reason was not Paraguayan pressure, but a Brazilian desire to shore up its southern neighbor: giving it a greater share of the dam revenues was easier than voting a foreign aid program.[222]

Though this was an improvement, economists conclude that in spite of the increase, Paraguay has suffered enormous economic losses by selling its energy to Brazil under these conditions. Recently, a report authored by Toledano and Maennling compared the wholesale price of electricity purchased by distributors in one domestic city's market (São Paulo). Though this economic analysis does not consider the variability for the rent of water applicable to the case, they used the data provided by the Central Bank of Paraguay for what they received in compensation, and concluded that the loss to Paraguay for selling its energy at the price determined by the Itaipu Treaty of 1973 was about US$748.6 million for 2012 alone.[223] This is 2.8 times as much as the total public works budget, and 746 times as much as the total energy budget of Paraguay. Clearly this issue needs to be addressed, since it is still the case that Paraguay is not using more of its hydroelectric energy rather than selling it to Brazil because it lacks the infrastructure and has difficulties financing improvements to infrastructure.[224]

---

220 Exchange of Notes, 28 January 1986. A factor of adjustment based on the year 1986 is also applied.

221 Exchange of Notes No. 4/09 dated September 2009, transcribed into Paraguayan Law No. 3923 dated 18 November 2009.

222 N. Maurer, *The Empire Trap* (Princeton University Press, 2013), at 447.

223 Toledano & Maennling, *supra* note 219.

224 For instance, to build a transmission line of 500 kV, Paraguay had to request financing from Brazil. *See* Memorandum of Understanding between Brazil and Paraguay, 28 June 2007; *see also* the statements of former Director General of Itaipu (Paraguay) in C. Mateo Balmelli, *Itaipu: Una Reflexión Etico-politíca Sobre el Poder* (Santillana SA, 2011).

There remain, however, contradictory opinions to those suggesting that the price of energy from Itaipu should be established pursuant to the current market value, the latter being the factor that could increase the amount of income for the countries. Zydan Soria, counsellor to the Brazilian Directorate of Itaipu,[225] has argued that market value as a parameter should not be used because the Itaipu project was a self-financed project, that is, all the generated debt is paid from the financial resources generated by the project itself.[226] And while it is true that any investment project should have an expected return, the Itaipu case is different.[227] Further, it should be noted that the portion of the price of energy allocated to royalties and compensation is very low in comparison to that of debt repayment (Table 4). Keeping the royalties low affects both Brazil and Paraguay, while the compensation item disadvantages Paraguay, because in practice, it is always Paraguay (a country with a population of 6.8 million) that sells its excess energy to Brazil (a country with a population of 207.7 million) for a fixed price, not in accordance with market value.

The infrastructure conditions of Paraguay when the Treaty was signed as compared to current times have, of course, changed. The Paraguayan national electricity company Asociación Nacional de Electricidad (ANDE) constructed a 500 kV transmission line, and has a project scheduled between 2016 and 2025 to develop more lines.[228] Recently, in October 2018, the Itaipu entity agreed to give some funds to ANDE to strengthen the electric distribution system through the purchase of 100 kV distribution converters.[229] It is still not comparable to the distribution lines that Brazil has (Figure 2). As Figure 2 shows, Brazil has eight 500 kV transmission lines, whereas Paraguay only has one, and the other four lines going to its territory are of much less capacity, 200 kV. This prevents Paraguay from using more hydroelectric energy.

225 Miguel Zydan Soria is a civil engineer and has worked for the Brazilian side of Itaipu for 24 years. Formerly he worked for Furnas Centrais Eletricas SA, a private Brazilian electricity entity, and was in charge of the Itaipu transmission system. At Itaipu, he has been Superintendent of the Environment, Planning and Control, was in charge of the Organizational Development Program, Corporate Process Coordination among others. He advises the Brazilian Directors of Itaipu.

226 It might be argued that if Brazil gets more energy, then it will pay more of this debt; however, since a Brazilian government controlled entity is also the main creditor, all the money simply flows back to Brazil. This is not the case for Paraguay.

227 Attempts to recover the full cost would entail having the debt paid first, and then pay dividends to the shareholders, which was not done in the case of Itaipu. Throughout the implementation of the Treaty, shareholders were paid dividends before the debt was paid off.

228 ANDE, *supra* note 181. *See also* Figure 2.

229 Agreement between ANDE and Itaipu to Strengthen the Distribution System, 12 October 2018.

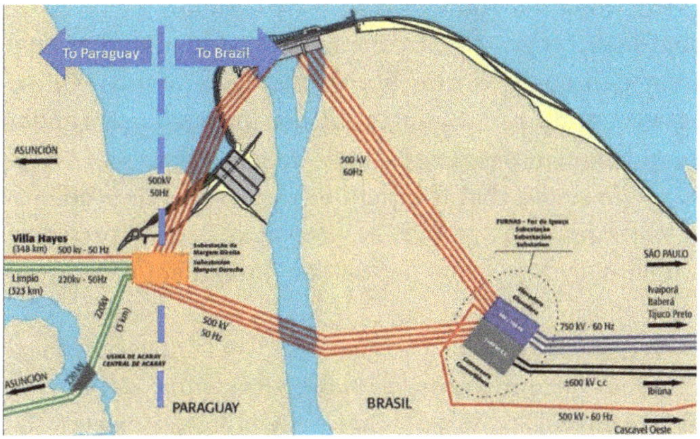

FIGURE 2 Difference in transmission line capacity between Paraguay and Brazil
SOURCE: ITAIPU BINACIONAL 'ITAIPU TRANSMISSIONS SYSTEM', GRAPH CONTAINED IN THE ITAIPU ENTITY'S DATABASE

Thus, royalties and compensation adjusted to market values are important considerations because they are sources of revenue. Paraguay still struggles with financing new transmission lines and improving existing ones; in other words, to use more clean and renewable energy, it will be necessary to improve the infrastructure.[230]

Adopting policies open to international financing could improve Paraguay's situation. World Bank or alternative foreign sources of financing to develop infrastructure could improve Paraguay's ability to use more hydroelectric energy. History has demonstrated how a closed policy for financing has not proven efficient. Considering that Paraguay is one of the friendliest investors with regard to the environment in the region and that there are so many options to finance renewable energy projects, the climate for international financing is propitious. As a result, Paraguay would benefit from the sustainable development effects resulting from its increased use of hydropower and suppression of biomass energy consumption.

---

230 There are, however, plans to build more transmission lines. See ANDE, Master Plan 2017. According to the 2017 budget report, the Public Works Ministry has a budget of US$266 million per year, and only US$1 million from that is assigned to the Sub-Secretary of Energy Office. To compare this with other sectors, the national health budget of the country was US$400 million per year (amounts given in approximation and upon variabilities of conversion exchange rates). See Paraguayan General Budget Law No. 5554/2017. With the agreement between ANDE and Itaipu Binacional signed in October 2018, ANDE received US$30 million to strengthen the distribution system.

4.1.3 The Lack of an Impartial Third Party to Solve Disputes

Although international law recognizes that companies of an international legal nature can be created through instruments like treaties, Clarence Wilfred Jenks, international lawyer and former director of the International Labour Organization, warned of a hidden danger in establishing companies of an international legal nature. He stated that for them to work, the independence of such entities must be guaranteed and that they must not cede to pressures or restrictions that would make the entity become an instrument of political control of one state over another.[231]

The Itaipu entity was created so that the two countries would not be involved in the administration of the dam and the power plant, for example, it would be the entity that would take out the loans required for the project. However, the Treaty establishes that this international company will have two shareholders, the two states' national electrical companies, ANDE and Eletrobras.

The entity's governing body comprises an Administrative Council and an Executive Board. The Administrative Council is composed of 12 representatives. Six will be appointed by the Government of Brazil, of which one will be designated by the Foreign Affairs Ministry and two by Eletrobras; similarly, six will be appointed by the Government of Paraguay, of which one will be designated by the Foreign Affairs Ministry and two by ANDE. The Board of Directors will only offer advice and no vote.[232] Thus, all major decisions and conduct of business of the entity lies in the hands of the Administrative Council, whose makeup is determined entirely by the national governments (which also own/control Eletrobras and ANDE, respectively). All of this politicizes the entity.

This is not necessarily a disadvantage, except that the Itaipu Treaty expressly establishes that any dispute should be resolved by diplomatic means only.[233] The same provision also states that these diplomatic means "shall not delay or interrupt the construction and/or operation of the hydroelectric development."[234] This wording resembles that of UNGA Resolution 2995 in regard to notifications, namely, "without this being construed as enabling each State to delay or impede the programmes and projects of exploration, exploitation and development of the natural resources of the States in whose territories such programmes and projects are carried out."[235]

The dam has been operational for 40 years, so the dispute settlement clause of the 1973 reference to diplomatic means might no longer reflect current legal

231 C.W. Jenks, *International Immunities* (London: Stevens & Sons Limited; New York: Oceana Publications, 1961).

232 Itaipu Treaty, *supra* note 101, art. 8, Annex A.

233 *Id.*, art. XXII.

234 *Id.*

235 GA Res 2995, *supra* note 97, para. 3.

approaches. Without a mechanism for resolving disputes by a third neutral party, conflicts may remain entirely political, bilateral, and subject to an asymmetrical scenario, given the imbalance of power between the two parties.[236]

Considering the key role of the Itaipu entity, it is important to note the lack of high-level coordination between decisions made by the Itaipu administration and the Department of Energy of either country. Though Brazil has a Ministry of Energy, and Paraguay a Sub-Secretary of Energy,[237] these institutions are completely independent and do not have an official process by which they coordinate their activities with those of the Itaipu entity, especially for Paraguay. Some of the Council decisions of the Itaipu entity have implemented regulations to the Treaty or had an effect on energy policies, but they did not go through parliamentary approval process.[238] Other areas of operation of the entity are not governed by the provisions of the Treaty. For instance, the Itaipu Treaty only refers to 18 turbines, but two more turbines were constructed for the Itaipu Dam. The binational entity is dividing the energy of those two extra turbines at the price that reflects its production costs and without following the provisions regarding the price of energy of the treaty.

Further, according to a former Director of the Itaipu entity, some expenses related to 'social' contributions of the entity to the Government of Paraguay have also been included in the price of energy. Although it is primarily the entity that releases these funds, it is the final consumer that pays for such expenses.[239] A treaty, and any modification to it, necessarily needs parliamentary approval in most South American legal orders. Though clearly such coordination takes place given the shared state interests and ownership of the project and use of a shared international river, having further provisions regulating this area in the treaty or in domestic laws would be beneficial.

236 For instance, a former Paraguayan Director of the Itaipu entity, Carlos Mateo writes in his memoirs about some of the disagreements he had while discussing project plans with his Brazilian counterpart. He reports that projects that were proposed to use the entity's fund to invest in infrastructure in Paraguay to optimize the energy consumption of Itaipu were denied, while at the same meetings, projects to give funds to a football team in Foz do Iguazu, Brazil, in order for them to qualify in the first division in the State of Parana were approved. Mateo Balmelli, *supra* note 224.

237 There has been some discussion about creating a Ministry of Energy in the Paraguayan Congress. Decree No. 6092, 10 October 2016, which approves the Paraguayan Energy Policy mentions this as a core aim that must be achieved in establishing an energy policy.

238 For example, the Annex C Regulation and the implementation of tariffs did not have parliamentary approval.

239 See the statement of the former Director of the Itaipu entity, Dr. Carlos Mateo Balmelli, in Mateo Balmelli, *supra* note 224, at Part V, 'La Disputa por Itaipu. Encuentros, Desencuentros y Propuestas', section 'La Posición Brasileña.'

Part 5: Disputes Relating to International Watercourses Decided by the International Court of Justice

Two key disputes concerning international watercourses that reached the International Court of Justice (ICJ) after the 1970s strengthen the arguments as to why international water and environmental law developments are important for the adaptation of bilateral treaties. Both cases are concerned with existing bilateral treaties over non-navigational uses of international watercourses. The aim is to see how the court interpreted the developments in international water law and international environmental law described above. As we shall see, these cases demonstrate the strong interconnections between water law and environmental protection, making it ever so difficult to separate these two areas from one another.

5.1 *The 1997 Gabčíkovo-Nagymaros Case*

In 1997, the Gabčíkovo-Nagymaros Project Case between Hungary and Czechoslovakia (Slovakia) was decided four months after the UN Watercourses Convention was adopted. The ICJ explicitly referred to the Convention in its judgment.[240]

The dispute concerned the rights of riparian states over the Danube River, a shared international watercourse and boundary between the two countries. They had signed the 1977 treaty by which they would jointly construct and operate the Gabčíkovo-Nagymaros system of locks (for a dam) in both countries; the project was a "single and indivisible operational system of works."[241] The joint investment was aimed at "the production of hydroelectricity, the improvement of navigation on the relevant section of the Danube and the protection of the areas along the banks against flooding ... the contracting parties undertook to ensure that the quality of water in the Danube was not impaired as a result of the Project, and that compliance with the obligations for the protection of nature arising in connection with the construction and operation of the System of Locks would be observed."[242]

During the construction phase of the larger project, Hungary decided to suspend works at Nagymaros, citing economic viability and preservation of the

240 *Case Concerning the Gabčíkovo-Nagymaros Project (Hungary/Slovakia)*, Judgment, ICJ Reports 1997, 7.

241 The project would consist of the Dunakility dam, the bypass canal and the two series of locks at Gabčíkovo and Nagymaros jointly owned by the contracting parties in equal measure. *Id.*, para. 18.

242 *Id.*, para. 15.

environment among their concerns.[243] The Government of Hungary commissioned further studies in this regard. The studies were concluded, and although there were some reassurances given to Slovakia that the project would continue, Hungary later said that the scientific studies could not guarantee that the environmental risks of the project could be handled given the construction plans. By 1989, Hungary proposed to Czechoslovakia a draft treaty completing the Gabčíkovo Dam in exchange for guarantees concerning the protection of the environment. But construction of the Nagymaros Dam was abandoned; subsequently, Hungary gave notice of termination of the 1977 Treaty.[244] As a consequence, Czechoslovakia put the 'Variant C' into operation, that is, works that effectively diverted the river into their territory.

The case definitely denoted a situation where Hungary saw itself affected by the uses of an international river shared with Slovakia, even though both countries had an international treaty concerning the matter.[245] The environmental concern was that the project would impair the quality of the water of the river in the long term. Hungary justified the decision for suspending or abandoning the project as an ecological necessity. Slovakia contended this and invoked the ecological studies made to that effect. It did not deny that were environmental risks, but argued that these risks could have been handled. Slovakia also denied breaching the Treaty in terms of protection of the environment and said that the environmental protection should be left up to both parties, depending of the location of the works.[246]

To decide the case, the Court took into consideration the Treaty, then international law, and thirdly local custom.[247] Regarding the suspension of works, the Court said that Hungary could not abandon its work "for which it was still responsible at Nagymaros and at Dunakiliti" and that the effect of this was that it rendered impossible the "accomplishment of the system of works that the Treaty expressly described as 'single and indivisible'." The Court found that the state of necessity claimed by Hungary did not allow it to suspend and abandon the project in 1989 because they had not shown any grave and imminent peril that Hungary could only avoid by abandonment. Thus, the obligations under the 1977 Treaty were still binding. However, the Court also stated that Hungary would

243 *Id.*, para. 31.

244 Both projects at Gabčíkovo and Nagymaros were considered part of the same 'system of works'.

245 Gabčíkovo -Nagymaros Case, *supra* note 240.

246 *Id.*, paras. 43–44.

247 This approach was followed in the Gabčíkovo -Nagymaros Case, *id.*, in 1997, as well as the Pulp Mills Case in 2010, *infra*.

not incur any international responsibility by acting as it did, but such state of necessity would not exempt it from compensating its partner.[248]

It should be noted, however, that the Court stated that "[t]he court has no difficulty in acknowledging that the concerns expressed by Hungary for its natural environment in the region affected by the Gabčíkovo-Nagymaros Project related to an 'essential interest' of that State."[249] The Court also recalled the ICJ's advisory opinion in Legality of the Threat or Use of Nuclear Weapons, in which it is stated that "[t]he existence of the general obligation of States to ensure that activities within their jurisdiction and control respect the environment of other States or of areas beyond national control is now part of the corpus of international law relating to the environment."[250] Note here, the importance of principle 21 of the 1972 Stockholm Declaration and the principle 2 of the Rio Declaration, and how the norm that contained in these non-binding instruments was considered customary international law.

The application of the principle of equitable and reasonable uses of international rivers was considered by the court when analyzing whether Slovakia acted lawfully when carrying on with the works in 1991, after Hungary had suspended the works on 1989. The Court found that Slovakia was entitled to proceed in November 1991, insofar as it confined itself to finalizing certain works, but that it was not entitled to initiate new works from October 1992. The ICJ noted that the Danube was a shared international watercourse and an international boundary river to which the principle of perfect equality between riparian states applied. Therefore, any unilateral action of one country (Czechoslovakia) to divert its waters deprived the other country (Hungary) of a right to a reasonable and equitable share of the uses of the watercourse.[251]

To reach this conclusion the Court noted the vast investments that had already been made, and that the construction project at Gabčíkovo and related works was mostly finished. Thus, not using the system would incur financial losses. However, it also noted that doing so could have given rise to serious environmental problems. The Court concluded that "Czechoslovakia, in putting Variant C into operation, was not applying the 1977 Treaty but, on the contrary, violated certain of its express provisions, and, in doing so, committed an internationally wrongful act."[252] But the Court then assessed whether or not

248 *Id.*, paras. 48,54 and 57.

249 *Id.*, para. 53.

250 *Legality of the Threat or Use of Nuclear Weapons*, Advisory Opinion, ICJ Reports 1996, 241–242, at para. 29.

251 Gabčíkovo-Nagymaros Case, *supra* note 240.

252 *Id.*, para. 78. Czechoslovakia had argued that the Variant C was equivalent to fulfilling what Hungary agreed to do under the treaty and failed to do, but the Variant C effectively

the wrongfulness could be precluded due to Hungary's failure to comply with its obligation under international law (a justifiable countermeasure). The Court found that for a countermeasure to be justifiable, it must be directed against the state, the injured state must have called upon the state committing the wrongful act to discontinue its wrongful conduct and "that the effects of the countermeasure must be commensurate with the injury suffered, taking account of the rights in question."[253]

On this point the Court stressed the principles of the 1997 UN Watercourses Convention.

> The Court considers that Czechoslovakia, by unilaterally assuming control of a shared resource, and thereby depriving Hungary of its right to an equitable and reasonable share of the natural resources of the Danube — with the continuing effects of the diversion of these waters on the ecology of the riparian area the Szigetköz — failed to respect the proportionality which is required by international law.[254]

Although Hungary originally agreed to some diversion of the Danube under the original plan, this agreement could not be interpreted as authorizing Czechoslovakia "to proceed with a unilateral diversion of this magnitude without Hungary's consent."[255] Therefore, the Court ruled that such action was neither proportionate nor lawful.

Further to emphasizing the 'basic right' of equitable and reasonable sharing of the international watercourse to decide on the case,[256] the Court also pointed to the consideration of protecting the environment. The case has thus been referred to as showing the integration of environmental protection and economic development.[257]

Hungary claimed that the prevention of damage pursuant to the precautionary principle has evolved into an *erga omnes* obligation, and that this justified Hungary's decision to terminate the Treaty. On the other hand, Slovakia claimed that none of the developments in environmental law gave

---

meant an appropriation of approximately 80 percent of the river by Czechoslovakia. The Court said that the Treaty's consent rested on Hungary's equitable and reasonable use of the river.

253 *Id.*, paras. 83–85.

254 *Id.*, para. 85.

255 *Id.*, para. 86.

256 *Id.*, para. 47.

257 Birnie et al., *supra* note 16 at 117.

rise to norms of *jus cogens* that would override the Treaty. However, the Court noted that

> newly developed norms of environmental law are relevant for the implementation of the Treaty and that the parties could, by agreement, incorporate them through the application of Articles 15, 19 and 20 of the Treaty ... By inserting these evolving provisions in the Treaty, the parties recognized the potential necessity to adapt the Project. Consequently, *the Treaty is not static, and is open to adapt to emerging norms of international law*. By means of Articles 15 and 19, new environmental norms can be incorporated in the Joint Contractual Plan.[258]

The Court also commented that this was a joint responsibility.

Further, the Court remarked on the evolution of norms:

> The Court is mindful that, in the field of environmental protection, vigilance and prevention are required on account of the often-irreversible character of damage to the environment and of the limitations inherent in the very mechanism of reparation of this type of damage.
>
> Throughout the ages, mankind has, for economic and other reasons, constantly interfered with nature. In the past, this was often done without consideration of the effects upon the environment. Owing to new scientific insights and to a growing awareness of the risks for mankind — for present and future generations — of pursuit of such interventions at an unconsidered and unabated pace, new norms and standards have been developed, set forth in a great number of instruments during the last two decades. Such new norms have to be taken into consideration, and such new standards given proper weight, not only when States contemplate new activities but also when continuing with activities begun in the past. This need to reconcile economic development with protection of the environment is aptly expressed in the concept of sustainable development.
>
> For the purposes of the present case, this means that the Parties together should look afresh at the effects on the environment of the operation of the Gabčíkovo power plant.[259]

---

258 Emphasis added. Articles 15 and 19 of the 1977 Treaty provided that the work on the dam should not impair the quality of the water in the Danube and that the parties would ensure compliance with the obligation for the protection of nature. *Id.*, para. 112.

259 *Id.*, para. 140.

Nonetheless, the Court noted that it is up to states, not the Court, to reach a decision on how to go forward with the project.

> It is not for the Court to determine what shall be the final result of these negotiations to be conducted by the Parties. It is for the Parties themselves to find an agreed solution that takes account of the objectives of the Treaty, which must be pursued in a joint and integrated way, as well as the norms of international environmental law and the principles of the law of international watercourses.[260]

The Court also reinforced the principle of good faith to achieve the purpose of the Treaty.[261] In regard to reparation, the Court said that reparation, which entailed 'wiping out' the consequences of the illegal act, would be done if the parties resumed their cooperation in the utilization of the shared water resources of the Danube, while developing it and protecting the watercourse in an equitable and reasonable manner.[262] Overall, the Court found that both parties had violated the Treaty with their actions and both had the duty to compensate each other for these violations and to cooperate further in developments on their shared watercourse.

5.2 *The 2010 Pulp Mills Case*

In 2010, the ICJ issued its judgment on the Pulp Mills Case concerning a dispute between Argentina and Uruguay over activities on the River Uruguay, a boundary river between both countries.[263] Uruguay had initiated construction and commissioning of two pulp mills on the River Uruguay. Argentina claimed that such activities would have effects on the water quality of the River Uruguay and on areas affected by the river. The case dealt with the law of treaties, international organizations, and international watercourses law. The Court remarked on general principles of international watercourses and its connection to the environment.

The legal framework for this case was provided by a treaty, known as the Montevideo Treaty, entered into by both countries that detailed the regime for using the river through a statute.[264] The statute was adopted to establish "the joint machinery necessary for the optimum and rational utilization of the river Uruguay, in strict observance of the rights and obligations arising

260 *Id.*

261 *Id.*, para. 142.

262 *Id.*, para. 150.

263 *Pulp Mills on the River Uruguay (Argentina v. Uruguay)*, Judgment, 20 April 2010, ICJ Reports 2010, 14.

264 Statute of the River Uruguay, 26 February 1975 [hereinafter 1975 Statute].

from the treaties and other international agreements in force for each of the parties."[265] Argentina claimed that by engaging in constructing pulp mills as planned, Uruguay was breaching procedural and substantive obligations of the treaty.[266] The procedural obligations identified included proper notification regarding activities affecting use of the river and the obligation to cooperate. The substantive obligations mainly dealt with the equitable and reasonable use of the shared resource and protection of the environment.[267] The principle of notification and its relevance in the uses of international watercourses was remarked upon. It was in this connection that the obligation to cooperate between riparian states so as to prevent environmental harm was also highlighted. The Court noted that the "procedural obligations of informing, notifying and negotiating constitute an appropriate means" to achieve objectives of reasonable and equitable uses of the shared resources. It continued, however, that "these obligations are all the more vital when a shared resource is at issue … which can only be protected through close and continuous cooperation between the riparian States."[268]

In regard to environmental protection, the Court noted the principle of prevention as customary international law, observing that "it has its origin in the due diligence that is required of a state in its territory."[269] In this regard, it stated an important legal basis for due diligence in preventing transboundary environmental damage, and, as before, remarked on the settled principle:

> A State is thus obliged to use all the means at its disposal in order to avoid activities which take place in its territory, or in any area under its jurisdiction, causing significant damage to the environment of another State.

265 The Treaty Concerning the Boundary Constituted by the River Uruguay (Montevideo Treaty), 7 April 1961 established the River Uruguay as their boundary river. Article 7 provided for a statute to determine the regime of use of the river. Pursuant to that article, the 1975 Statute, *id.*, was entered into by both countries. See also Pulp Mills Case, *supra* note 263, para. 26.

266 For a detailed summary see P. Sands & J. Peel, with A. Fabra and R. MacKenzie (eds.), *Principles of International Environmental Law* (3rd edition, Cambridge University Press, 2003), at 330; Pulp Mills Case, *id.*

267 The alleged breaches concerned specifically the 'optimum and rational utilization of the river', the 'obligation to coordinate measures to avoid changes in the ecological balance of the river', the 'obligation to ensure that the management of the soil and woodland does not impair the regime of the river or the quality of the waters', and the 'obligation to prevent pollution and preserve the aquatic environment'. Pulp Mills Case, *supra* note 263, at 169–266.

268 Pulp Mills Case, *supra* note 263, para. 81. In this case specifically, the Court referred to the objective of Article 1 of the 1975 Statute.

269 *Id.*, para. 101.

> This Court has established that this obligation 'is now part of the corpus of international law relating to the environment'.[270]

In this regard, as the Court mentioned, the obligation to inform triggers the obligation to cooperate, which is necessary to fulfil the obligation of prevention.[271] The obligation to notify is crucial for enabling consultations and assessing any risks that such planned activities may impose. In this way the parties could eliminate or minimize the risks, and environmental impact assessments were one way to achieve this goal. But the Court also observed that such notification "must take place before the State concerned decides on the environmental viability of the plan, taking due account of the environmental impact assessment submitted to it."[272] Further, the procedure stated in the international treaty has priority over any provisions in domestic legislation.[273]

The Montevideo Treaty had a dispute settlement provision regarding interpretation and application of the treaty, pursuant to which, failing negotiations, the matter should be submitted to the ICJ. The Court found that this provision gave jurisdiction to the Court, but it did not mean that the Court should have decided on the authorization of the planned activities. It concluded, "[c]onsequently, the State initiating the plan may, at the end of the negotiation period, proceed with construction at its own risk."[274]

As for the substantial claims, the general principles of international watercourses law regarding the uses of the river in an equitable and reasonable manner were considered together with other factors. In this case, the 'optimum and rational utilization of the river' required balancing with its use for economic and commercial activities, as well as environmental protection.[275] The Court pointed to

> the need to reconcile the varied interests of riparian states in a transboundary context and in particular in the use of a shared natural resource, but also the need to strike a balance between the use of the waters and the protection of the river consistent with the objective of sustainable development.... The Court wishes to add that such utilization could not be considered to be equitable and reasonable if the interests of the other

270 *Id.*, quoting Legality of the Threat or Use of Nuclear Weapons, Advisory Opinion, ICJ Reports 1996 (I), 242, para. 29.

271 *Id.*, paras. 102 and 113.

272 *Id.*, para. 120.

273 *Id.*, para. 121, citing Article 27 of the Vienna Convention on the Law of Treaties.

274 *Id.*, para. 154 and summary at 15.

275 *Id.*, para. 175.

> riparian State in the shared resource and the environmental protection of the latter were not taken into account..... [T]his interconnectedness between equitable and reasonable utilization of a shared resource and the balance between economic development and environmental protection is the essence of sustainable development.[276]

The Court found that Uruguay did not breach this substantive obligation in that regard.

In regard to the obligation to prevent any transboundary pollution to change the ecological balance of the river, the view of the Court was that such an obligation relies on both parties' actions. The Court found that by establishing a regulatory framework and by exercising due diligence with the measures to be implemented, the parties were complying with this obligation. It concluded that there was no evidence of Uruguay refusing to cooperate in this regard.[277]

As concerns the obligation to protect the environment and prevent pollution, the Court remarked again on the principle of ensuring that activities within their jurisdiction and control respect the environment of other states.[278] Furthermore, it regarded the importance of due diligence. The Court stated:

> Thirdly, the obligation to 'preserve the aquatic environment, and in particular to prevent pollution by prescribing appropriate rules and measures' is an obligation to act with due diligence in respect of all activities which take place under the jurisdiction and control of each party. It is an obligation which entails not only the adoption of appropriate rules and measures, but also a certain level of vigilance in their enforcement and the exercise of administrative control applicable to public and private operators, such as the monitoring of activities undertaken by such operators, to safeguard the rights of the other party.[279]

The Court further commented,

> In this sense, the obligation to protect and preserve, under Article 41 (*a*) of the Statute, has to be interpreted in accordance with a practice, which in recent years has gained so much acceptance among States that it may now be considered a requirement under general international law to

276 *Id.*, para. 177.

277 *See* Sands and Peel, *supra* note 266, at 331; Pulp Mills Case, *id.*, paras. 184 and 185.

278 Legality of the Threat or Use of Nuclear Weapons, *supra* note 250, para. 29.

279 Pulp Mills Case, *supra* note 263, para. 197 and summary at 18.

> undertake an environmental impact assessment where there is a risk that the proposed industrial activity may have a significant adverse impact in a transboundary context, in particular, on a shared resource. Moreover, due diligence, and the duty of vigilance and prevention which it implies, would not be considered to have been exercised, if a party planning works liable to affect the régime of the river or the quality of its waters did not undertake an environmental impact assessment on the potential effects of such works.[280]

The Court found that Uruguay did not breach the obligation to prevent environmental harm in the Treaty, due to the environmental impact assessment provided by Uruguay and the fact that Uruguay used the best alternative technology standards to test any harm. Sands and Peel, however, have pointed out the dissenting opinion of two judges regarding the difference in the scientific methodology used for assessing the pollution.[281]

Overall, the Court found that Uruguay breached its procedural obligations (notification and consultation), but did adhere to its obligation of due diligence. The Court found that Uruguay had not breached the substantive obligations regarding the protection and preservation of the environment because it had provided an environmental impact assessment.

5.3 *Remarks about the Legal Developments and the Adaptation of Treaties*

The development of the law reflected in the international conventions, international environmental laws, state practice, and the application of the key principles in settling international disputes offer important lessons concerning international watercourses law. We have seen how, even though states have entered into a bilateral treaty over the use of an international watercourse, international courts and tribunals interpret them in light of developments in both the law of international watercourses and international environmental law.

In particular, in the Gabčíkovo Case, the ICJ analyzed provisions of the 1977 Treaty which provided that the works should not impair the quality of the water in the Danube (Article 15), and that the parties, through the contractual plan, would ensure compliance with the obligation to protect nature (Article 19). These provisions were sufficient for the Court to say that the Treaty was "not static, and is open to adapt to emerging norms of international law."

---

280 *Id.*, para. 204 and summary at 18.

281 Sands and Peel, *supra* note 266, at 332–333.

Similarly, in the Pulp Mills case, the ICJ pointed out that practices that have gained acceptance among states in the area of environmental protection, even when not included in the provisions in a statute between the parties, must also be taken into account when addressing prevention of transboundary environmental damage.

International environmental law now places responsibility on states to not cause damage to the environment when exploiting resources. There is also the general obligation of states to ensure that activities within their jurisdiction and control respect the environment of other states (and areas beyond national control), principles that were established in the 1972 Stockholm Declaration and the 1992 Rio Declaration. These principles were reaffirmed by the ICJ in the 1996 Legality of the Threat or Use of Nuclear Weapons Case, the 1997 Gabčíkovo Case, and the 2010 Pulp Mills Case. In all of these cases the Court stated that these principles now form the corpus of international law. When we describe the uses of international watercourses, these provisions are relevant, as the principles of reasonable and equitable use, as discussed above, comprise the determination of no harm to other riparians.

Thus, for the development of international watercourses and to respect the principle of no harm, environmental protection is crucial. States must notify other states of activities that utilize shared resources that can affect the environment. Providing such information is necessary to prevent environmental damage. Timely notification, information exchange, and consultation with affected states have all been established as key principles under environmental conventions.

As shown in the discussion above on the ICJ cases, an international tribunal is not the final decision-maker authorizing activity when negotiations have failed and the state may carry out proposed activities. It is established in international law that "an obligation to negotiate does not imply an obligation to reach an agreement."[282] This is consistent with the reference to consultation in the 2001 ILC Articles on Transboundary Harm, which establishes that "the State of origin shall nevertheless take into account the interests of the State likely to be affected in case it decides to authorize the activity to be pursued, without prejudice to the rights of any State likely to be affected."[283] As established by the Pulp Mills Case, considerations of due diligence are crucial in this regard.

---

282 *Railway traffic between Lithuania and Poland,* Advisory Opinion, 1931, PCIJ (series A/B) No 42 (15 October 1931), at 116; reinforced in *Obligation to Negotiate Access to the Pacific Ocean (Bolivia v Chile)*, Judgment, ICJ Report 2018.

283 2001 Draft Articles, *supra* note 133, art. 9(3).

There should be no confusion, however, between consultation and negotiation as steps to be taken to ensure reasonable and equitable use of a watercourse, and the negotiation stages in dispute settlement mechanisms. The former concerns obligations for the use of an international watercourse, the latter concerns an existing dispute and the particular stages to resolve it, failing which, parties proceed to the stage of submission of the dispute to a neutral third party.[284] In the practice of reasonable and equitable use of international watercourses, for consultation and negotiations to happen, there must be good faith, trust, and confidence: "One of the basic principles governing the creation and performance of legal obligations, whatever their source, is the principle of good faith. Trust and confidence are inherent in international co-operation."[285]

The requirement of cooperation among states in the utilization of international watercourses remains one of the most complex issues in the international system. It is clear from the discussion above surrounding the practices of the use of international watercourses that riparian states are obliged to take particular actions, but these actions can have ramifications. For instance, the action of giving notification, or informing about particular projects or uses in an international watercourse are a trigger to cooperation. Cooperation involves practices which aim at reasonably and equitably using the international watercourse and preventing any harm. This exercise comes about only through consultation and negotiations over the particular uses of shared international watercourses. As pointed out by key scholars in the area,[286] cooperation, consultation, and negotiations must take place through affirmative action, for instance by due diligence practices, with the aim of mitigating or eliminating any risks associated with the uses of shared water resources that might cause significant damage to the other party (Figure 3). States may carry out their activities, having had consideration for affected states, which mitigates harm. If nevertheless harm occurs, then international responsibility may arise depending of the particular case.

---

284 In international arbitration, the separability principle is well-known, but it relates to the stages once a dispute exists. Cooperation is a substantial obligation and a dispute in that regard may overlap, but an act involving cooperation does not always need to involve a dispute. In Pulp Mills, the Court considered the right of veto in relation to the dispute settlement clause. The right to veto to which international watercourses law refers to is consultation on the uses of the river and how a party can carry out developments. See Pulp Mills Case, *supra* note 263, paras. 151–152.

285 *Nuclear Tests (Australia v France)*, Judgment, ICJ Reports 1974, 268, paras. 46 and 49; *see also Border and Transborder Armed Actions (Nicaragua v Honduras)*, Jurisdiction and Admissibility, Judgment, ICJ Reports 1988, 105, para. 94.

286 McCaffrey 2001, *supra* note 125; McCaffrey 2007, *supra* note 9; Birnie et al., *supra* note 16.

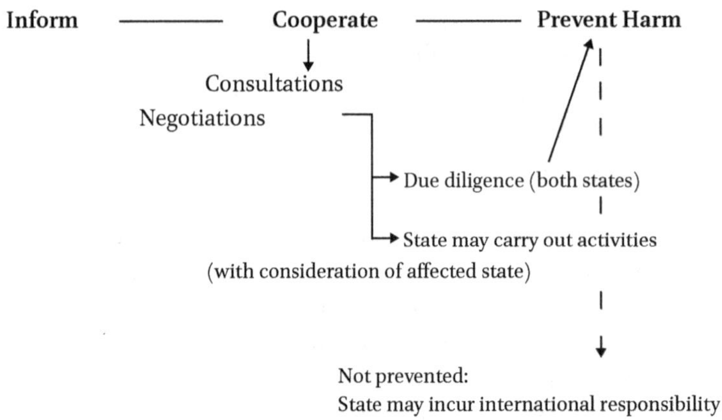

FIGURE 3 Cooperation process in the utilization of international watercourses
SOURCE: CREATED BY THE AUTHOR

The development of international water law is comprised by formally binding as well as by non-binding sources of law. General principles that evolved from non-binding instruments have proven to be of great importance. Principles such as the precautionary principles, according to which the polluter pays, and that of common but differentiated responsibilities, have all evolved from either UN environmental forums or soft law treaties. As Birnie, Boyle and Redgewell note, the influence of such instruments depends on their interpretation in accordance with the Vienna Convention on the Law of Treaties.[287] When these principles influence state practice and these are coupled with *opinio juris*, they lay down parameters that affect the way courts decide cases: "They may lack the supposedly harder edge of a 'rule' or 'obligation', but they should not be confused with 'non-binding' or emerging law."[288]

International law covering international watercourses is much more advanced today. This analysis has attempted to show some important developments in this process. Multilateral conventions, regional, and bilateral treaties can all be part of general agreements on the uses of international watercourses. Multilateral treaties that are in force contain general norms, but there could be regional agreements that contain specific norms regarding the particularities of specific geographic locations. In this sense both general and specific norms resulting from different types of agreements could complement each other. In this regard, Boisson de Chazournes mentions the importance of

287 Vienna Convention on the Law of Treaties, 23 May 1969, art. 31(3).
288 Birnie et al., *supra* note 16 at 28.

harmonization: "The harmonization of water practices and the relation between universal norms and specific instruments on transboundary water resources is apparent and should be promoted further in a mutually supportive way."[289] With these considerations in mind, states can prolong a treaty in its current form even when the treaty states a time for the treaty to be renegotiated but it would be wise to take the opportunity of renegotiation to be mindful of the changes in international law that have occurred since the treaty was first signed. For the best way to honor a treaty, and the relationship that it creates between states, could be to adapt it to the current developments of international law.

Part 6: Conclusion

The adaptation of treaties to developments in international law not only fosters cooperation in the utilization of international watercourses, but also sustainable development. Bilateral watercourse treaties that were signed in the 1970s, implemented with no subsequent legal revision, are likely lacking the alignment needed to maintain long-lasting sustainable practices. This case study discusses these challenges, looking at the most important hydroelectric energy treaty in the South American region, the Itaipu Treaty. The Treaty's provisions concern the use of the Parana River to produce hydropower; thus, it is directly relevant to the international law on watercourses and environmental law. In particular, the development of international water law and its integration with international environmental law and climate change law will have implications for watercourses treaties. Treaties regarding the uses of international watercourses and those aimed at producing clean sources of energy will also impact state practice in these areas.

There are many reflections one could make based on this case study of the Itaipu Treaty. There are obvious interconnections with international water law and international environmental and climate change law in the implementation of the Itaipu Treaty. To begin with, the core principle of reasonable and equitable use of the international river might be affected by its provisions restricting third-party energy sales, fixing energy consumption indexes for 10 years, and adopting a compensation calculation that is not based on market value. When other countries with jurisdiction over the water basin that sources the river offer to purchase the energy at a much higher price, or having a

289 L. Boisson de Chazournes, *Fresh Water in International Law* (Oxford University Press, 2013), at 52.

price adjusted to market value, Paraguay, which is a land-locked and developing country, would have the possibility of obtaining more income to develop infrastructure needed to use more of its renewable energy, instead of obtaining its energy through biomass sources.

These treaty restrictions, which in practice only affect one of the parties, may negatively impact the exercise of equitable and reasonable use of international watercourses. The implementation of the Itaipu Treaty disregards factors such as the social and economic needs of states, the effects of the use in one watercourse state, the conservation, protection, development and economy of use of the water resource, and the comparable value of existing uses. This is a non-exhaustive list of factors that amount to use of watercourses in a reasonable and equitable manner. These factors are included in the UN Watercourses Convention and the 2001 ILC Articles on Transboundary Harm. In particular, they are connected to sustainable development agendas.

The implementation of the Itaipu Treaty, which relates to the use of clean and renewable energy, also goes in hand with reducing greenhouse emissions. However, the Itaipu Treaty entered into force before key conventions like the UN Watercourses Convention and international environmental agreements and climate change commitments like the Paris Agreement entered into force. Some of the provisions of the Itaipu Treaty have direct consequences on state practices, such as obtaining energy from the burning of wood, that need to be addressed. The effect of keeping energy generation sources from biomass, which contributes to deforestation, when renewable energy sources are available, endangers the watercourses and water basin ecosystems. In turn, the production of energy might also be affected. Technical studies have found stated that "if forest degradation continues at the rate seen during the 2000–2010 period, the *Itaipu dam* could probably be impacted operationally and economically from the short to middle term."[290] This would have an impact on both countries and eventually all others in the river basin.

However, there is a will arising from state practices and the Itaipu entity to meet such environmental and sustainable goals. For instance, the duty of 'social responsibility' has been incorporated in many of the plans of the Itaipu entity.[291] In March 2018, the Itaipu entity signed a partnership agreement with the UN Department of Economic and Social Affairs and during

290 Saenz, *supra* note 184. Emphasis added.

291 These are mentioned within the internal strategic plans of the Itaipu entity. The concept of social responsibility as one of the aims of the entity was established by an Exchange of Notes dated March 2005. *See* Mateo Balmelli, *supra* note 224, at Part V, 'La Disputa por Itaipu. Encuentros, Desencuentros y Propuestas', section 'La Posición Brasileña.'

the UN Climate Change conference (COP 24) in Poland in 2018 launched the 'Sustainable Water and Energy Solutions' Global Network to promote water and energy sustainability in support of the agenda for sustainable development.[292] Most countries, including Brazil and Paraguay, also have expressed their commitment to reducing greenhouse gasses in their respective National Determined Contributions.[293] These non-binding commitments are noteworthy, but it is also important for the states to re-examine the binding treaty provisions. Treaty restrictions that prevent state practices that support environmental-friendly policies could conflict with substantial international law obligations such as the equitable utilization principle and the obligation of no harm. The upcoming renegotiation of the Itaipu Treaty might mean that the issue of consultation rises again among riparians concerned about this international river, particularly if the use of the river is in any way affected by either a new agreement or if the environmental provisions are not revised.

The Itaipu Treaty does not expressly address environmental protection, but the preceding and subsequent agreements on the uses of the same international watercourse do mention environmental protection. The Cuenca del Plata Treaty regulates the use of the rivers and obliges state parties to protect the rivers of the basin. The Declaration of Asunción of 1971 expressly addresses the study and rules to prevent contamination of the rivers sourced by the La Plata basin (Resolution No. 23). Finally, the Tri-partite Agreement on the uses of the Parana River establishes provisions which expressly address the operations of Itaipu and the Cuenca del Plata Treaty. The Tri-partite Agreement calls for equitable and reasonable use of the river with the aim of preventing the contamination of the Parana River (Article 5(j)). More recently, these environmental protection commitments were reinforced with the Agreement on the Guarani Aquifer. Thus, the parties to the Itaipu Treaty may consider these legal developments specifically addressing the uses of the Parana River when renegotiating the Itaipu Treaty. Some of these developments are derived from the institutionalization and regulation of the Parana River. They should not be undermined, as they reflect the benefit from the shared exploitation of rivers.

It is also important to note the adaptation of the dispute settlement mechanism recommended for international watercourse agreements. The Itaipu Treaty limits dispute settlement to diplomatic negotiations and does not allow for arbitration or any other dispute settlement level or mechanism. In contrast,

---

292 For details of the Sustainable Water and Energy Solutions Partnership, *see* https://sustainabledevelopment.un.org/waterenergypartnership (last accessed 21 December 2018).

293 Countries' reports on their National Determined Contributions are published by the UNFCCC.

the recommendations from the earliest historic agreements on the topic, such as the 1899 Convention on the Pacific Settlement of International Disputes, have pointed out that "in questions of a legal nature, and especially in the interpretation or application of Intentional Conventions" arbitration is "the most effective, and at the same time the most equitable means of settling disputes *which diplomacy has failed to settle*."[294] Different stages in the settlement process include arbitration (third party neutral), which has been recommended in the UN Charter, the Helsinki Rules, and the UN Watercourses Convention. The latter includes a robust mechanism for settlement of disputes, which includes different stages to managing a dispute.[295] Such recommendations may be used to adapt these treaties in the spirit of following the principles of reasonable and equitable use of the international watercourses.

These legal and institutional developments also provide other advantages. The financing of international institutions and projects involves assessment of risks and due diligence requirements, and in addition to new forms of financing tailored for developing countries. For example, new financing mechanisms for new institutions created to promote the use of renewable energy favors developing countries. This is particularly relevant not only for Paraguay; on the contrary, it could be an advantage to both countries. Both Brazil and Paraguay could benefit from increased energy production from Itaipu. Other funding mechanisms such as the Global Environmental Facility or those established under the Kyoto Protocol promote financing for clean carbon projects. Using more renewable energy rather than biomass, as well as developing infrastructure further to transmit the energy produced at Itaipu to third countries in the region, could not only set an example, but by doing so, assist Brazil and Paraguay in meeting their international commitments, like those in the Paris Agreement.

Considering that the developments in international water and environmental law are now part of the corpus of international law, the consequences in terms of changes with regard to treaties, could be manifested in two ways. The changes could be either implicit or explicit.

An implicit change to a treaty could derive from what was discussed above concerning the settlement of international disputes. In the examples of the disputes that were submitted to the ICJ, in the Gabčíkovo Case, a treaty

294 Convention for the Pacific Settlement of International Disputes, 29 July 1899, art. 16 (emphasis added).

295 Article 33 of the UN Watercourses Convention, *supra* note 1, establishes that if a dispute is not resolved through negotiation, then the parties can use other means such as fact finding and arbitration. Its article 3 (2) states that parties to watercourse agreements may consider harmonizing such agreements with the basic principles of the convention.

concerning the uses of watercourses also existed, the Court pointed out how new norms and standards that have been developed for the protection of the environment must be considered not only in past developments on watercourses, but also in the continuation of operation of works such as dams. Similarly, in the Pulp Mills Case, the Court pointed out that environmental protection and prevention of transboundary damage are to be interpreted not only with what it is agreed to in an agreement or statute between the parties, but also through practices that have gained acceptance among states in the area of environmental protection. The Court further stated that given that these norms are part of international law, obligations to notify and enable consultation are part of the obligation to cooperate to prevent environmental damage. In this case, the Court also ruled that environmental effects must be monitored throughout the entire life of the project, reflecting the duty of states of due diligence practices to prevent environmental damage. In other words, even though the treaty text was not changed in either case, the meaning of the treaties had been changed implicitly by interpreting them in the light of developments in international law, and state practices concerning these activities might change after the decision of the Court. However, this implicit change presupposes the submission of disputes to an international adjudicator in order to have such effects.

An explicit change would occur if the treaty partners expressly changed the text of the treaty, which would be the most natural way for the Itaipu Treaty to incorporate developments in international law. In this regard, the adaptation and change of the text of watercourse treaties are not novel; in fact, there are many examples reflecting this practice.[296]

These legal considerations will be relevant for the renegotiation of treaties, even more so when the treaty has explicitly provided for its renegotiation, making it a material obligation between the parties.[297] The Itaipu Treaty contains an express provision to renegotiate the provisions regarding financial services, price, and management of the energy, 50 years after its conclusion. It will be up to the states to decide how to renegotiate and what to include in the objectives

---

296 For instance, the Southern African Development Community revised their 1995 Protocol on Shared Watercourses System in 2000; agreements regarding the Lake Victoria Basin, the Zambezi, the Nile Basin, and the Guarani Aquifer Agreement have also been instrumental in developing international water law and international environmental law.

297 The clause on renegotiation in the Itaipu Treaty makes it a material obligation for the parties, which differs considerably from the dispute that arose between Bolivia and Chile in which the ICJ had to assess the communication between the countries to determine whether these countries had an obligation to negotiate sovereign access to the Pacific. The Court found it did not. *See* Obligation to Negotiate Access to the Pacific Ocean, *supra* note 282.

of renegotiation. However, states should also be aware of legal developments and how they might impact the direction of negotiations, for example when considering the environmental protection of the river basin.

Although the Treaty has not yet been adapted to the latest developments in international law, the analysis of its implementation, which showed its effects on domestic energy policies, has shown why such adaptation might be useful. Such changes will uphold the same purposes for which the Treaty was entered into by the parties, in particular to promote the development of both countries.

Renegotiation of treaty provisions not only reflects the aim of the treaty partners who included such an explicit provision foreseeing change, but is also a key step in the process of cooperation. The alignment of treaty provisions to international standards is not only to the benefit of the treaty partners, they would also entail the protection of the water basin in the region, in this case, the source of the energy that has made the Itaipu endeavor successful. When the treaty partners include provisions regarding use of the international watercourses in an equitable and reasonable manner and with environmental protection considerations, and develop their policies in accordance with these principles, these treaty partners are fostering sustainable development for present and future generations by allowing them to keep using and enjoying the full potential of their natural resources.

At the beginning of this monograph the question was posed as to whether the recommendation of the UN Watercourses Convention to adapt watercourse agreements to follow the provisions of the Convention would bring about advantages to the treaty partners of such agreements. In light of the analysis here, this question can be answered with an unequivocal affirmation. One can confidently point out to states the advantages of adapting their treaties to the current standards of international law, particularly those important provisions concerning the uses of watercourses laid down in the UN Watercourses Convention.

Acknowledgements

My sincere thanks and appreciation to Dr. Salman M. A. Salman for undertaking so thoroughly the responsibilities of Editor-in-Chief for this monograph, and to the other members of the Editorial Board of Brill Research Perspectives in International Water Law. I thank the external peer reviewers, as well as the members of the intellectual community of Princeton University, the University of Oxford, and the University of Bonn for providing valuable feedback and comments that benefited the development and completion of this monograph.

Bibliography

Angstman, B. L., D. Clarke, B. G. Garth, D. Hooker, K. D. Knudsen, J. C. Noonan & B. H. Thompson, '*The Stockholm Conference: A Synopsis and Analysis*', 8 Stanford Journal of International Studies (1973): 31.

Asociación Nacional de Electricidad (ANDE), 'El Sector Eléctrico Paraguayo: Evolución y Desafíos de la ANDE', presentation, 26 May 2017.

Barberis, J. A., *Los Recursos Naturales Compartidos entre Estados y el Derecho Internacional* (Madrid: Editorial Tecnos, 1979).

Bertoni, G. T., *Geografia Economica del Paraguay* (Editorial Guarani, 1940).

Birnie, P., A. Boyle & C. Redgwell, *International Law and the Environment* (Oxford University Press, 2009).

Blanc, J., '*Itaipu's Forgotten History: The 1965 Brazil-Paraguay Border Crisis and the New Geopolitics of the Southern Cone*', 50 Journal of Latin American Studies (2017): 383–409.

Boisson de Chazournes, L., *Fresh Water in International Law* (Oxford University Press, 2013).

Caflisch, L., '*The Law of International Waterways and its Sources*', in R. St J. Macdonald (ed.), *Essays in Honour of Wang Tieya* (Kluwer: Martinus Nijhoff Publishers, 1994).

Caponera, D., *National and International Water Law and Administration* (Kluwer Law International, 2003).

Cardozo, E., *Los Derechos del Paraguay sobre los Saltos del Guaira* (Asunción: Talleres Gráficos, 1965).

Costantini, F. B., '*Itaipu y Yacyreta como Entidades, Sociedades o Corporaciones Públicas Internacionales*', Revista UCA (2007): 619–648.

Crawford, J., *Brownlies' Principles of Public International Law* (Oxford University Press, 2012).

da Rosa, E., '*Economics, Politics, and Hydroelectric Power: The Parana River Basin*', 18:3 Latin American Research Review (1983): 77–107.

Debernardi, E., *Apuntes para la Historia Política de Itaipu* (Editorial Grafica Continua, 1996).

Debernardi, E. 'Estrategia de Desarrollo en Condiciones de Oferta Abundante de Energía Eléctrica' IDB Minutes of Congress, 28 July–1 August 1980, Asunción, Paraguay.

Freestone, D., '*The United Nations Framework Convention on Climate Change. The Basis for the Climate Change Regime*', in C. P. Carlarne, K. Gray & R. Tarasofsky (eds.), *The Oxford Handbook of International Climate Change Law* (Oxford University Press, 2016).

Freestone, D., '*The International Climate Change Legal and Institutional Framework: An Overview*', in D. Freestone & C. Streck (eds.), *Legal Aspects of Carbon Trading* (Oxford University Press, 2009).

Germani, G. I., *Expropriados Terra e Agua: O Conflito de Itaipu* (Editora da ULBRA, 2003).

Godana, B., *Africa's Shared Water Resources* (London: Frances Pinter Publishers, 1985).

Harris, D., & S. Sivakumaran, *Cases and Materials on International Law* (Sweet and Maxwell, 2015).

International Law Association (ILA), Helsinki Rules on the Uses of the Waters of International Rivers, in *Report of the 52nd Conference* (Helsinki, 14–20 August 1966).

International Law Association (ILA), Berlin Rules on Water Resources, in *Report of the 71st Conference* (Berlin, 21 August 2004).

International Law Commission, Draft Articles on Prevention of Transboundary Harm from Hazardous Activities, in *Report of the International Law Commission on the work of its fifty-third session (23 April–1 June and 2 July–10 August 2001)*, UN Doc. A/56/10, extract from the Yearbook of the International Law Commission, 2001, Vol. II, Part Two.

Itaipu Binacional, '*Prestación de los Servicios de Electricidad y Bases Financieras: Compendio*' (Grafica Asuncena, 2003).

Jenks, C. W., *International Immunities* (London: Stevens & Sons Limited; New York: Oceana Publications, 1961).

Lammers, J., *Pollution of International Watercourses* (Hague/Dordrecht/Lancaster: Martinus Nijhoff, 1984).

Maurer, N., *The Empire Trap* (Princeton University Press, 2013).

MacDowell, J. '*A Politica do Brasil no Contexto de Tratado da Bacia do Prata*', 37 Revista Brasileira de Estudos Politicos (1973): 9–21.

Magalhaes, J., & J. A. Gueiros, *O Último Tenente* (São Paulo: Editora Record, 1996).

Malhi, Y., J. T. Roberts, R. A. Betts, T. J. Killeen, W. Li, & C. A. Nobre, '*Climate Change, Deforestation, and the Fate of the Amazon*', 319:5860 Science (2008): 169–172.

Mariotti, M., '*Posibilidades del Desarrollo de la Industria hidroeléctrica en el Paraguay*', I Revista de la Sociedad Científica del Paraguay (1925).

Martinez Adalid, J. O., '*La Controversia Argentina-Brasileña Sobre el Aprovechamiento Hidroeléctrico del Rio Paraná y el Acuerdo Tripartito de 1979*', XVII–XVIII Prudentia luris (1985–1986): 69–91.

Mateo Balmelli, C., *Itaipu, una reflexión ético-política sobre el poder* (Santillana SA, 2011).

Mbengue, M., '*A Model for African Shared Water Resources: The Senegal River Legal System*', 23:1 Review of European Community and International Environmental Law (2014): 59–66.

Mbengue, M., '*The Senegal River Legal Regime and Its Contribution to the Development of the Law of International Watercourses in Africa*', in L. Boisson de Chazournes, C. Leb & M. Tignino (eds.), *International Law and Freshwater: The Multiple Challenges* (Edward Elgar, 2013).

McCaffrey, S. C., '*The Contribution of the UN Convention on the Law of the Non-navigational Uses of International Watercourses*', 1:3/4 International Journal of Global Environmental Issues (2001): 250–263.

McCaffrey, S. C., *The Law of International Watercourses: Non-navigational Uses* (Oxford University Press, 2001).

McCaffrey, S. C., *The Law of International Watercourses* (2nd edition, Oxford University Press, 2007).

McCaffrey, S. C., & M. Sinjela, '*The 1997 United Nations Convention on International Watercourses*', 92:1 The American Journal of International Law (1998): 97–107.

Miller, R. A., '*Trail Smelter Arbitration*', Max Planck Encyclopedia of Public International Law (2007).

Nickson, A., '*The Itaipu Hydro-Electric Project: The Paraguayan Perspective*', 2:1 Bulletin of Latin American Research (1982): 1–20.

Odili, N. C., '*Shared Water Resources in West Africa*', 3:1 Brill Research Perspectives in International Water Law (2018): 1–98.

Potapov, P., M. C. Hansen, L. Laestadius, S. Turubanova, A. Yaroshenko, C. Thies & E. Esipova, '*The Last Frontiers of Wilderness: Tracking Loss of Intact Forest Landscapes from 2000 to 2013*', 3:1 Science Advances e1600821(2017).

Querol, M., '*Freshwater Boundaries Revisited*', 1:3 Brill Research Perspectives in International Water Law (2016): 1–89.

Ramirez, I., 'El Litigio Fronterizo con el Brasil: Desenmascaramiento de Itamarati', *Patria* (Asunción), 1966.

Ramos Gimenez, L., 'Sobre el Salto del Guaria al Oído de America', *Patria* (Asunción), 21 April 1966.

Sachs, J., L. Sachs, P. Toledano & N. Maennling, *Leveraging Paraguay's Hydropower for Sustainable Economic Development: Final Report* (Vale Columbia Center on Sustainable International Investment, November 2013).

Saenz, L., *Assessing Impacts of Deforestation in Itaipu's Dam Watershed in Paraguay* (World Resources Institute, July 2018).

Salman, S. M. A., '*The United Nations Watercourse Convention Ten Years Later: Why Has its Entry into Force Proven Difficult?*', 32:1 Water International (2007a): 1–15.

Salman, S. M. A., '*The Helsinki Rules, the UN Watercourses Convention and the Berlin Rules: Perspectives on International Water Law*', 23:4 Water Resources Development (2007b): 625–640.

Salman, S. M. A., '*Entry into Force of the UN Watercourses Convention: Why Should It Matter?*', 31:1 International Journal of Water Resources Development (2014): 4–16.

Sands, P., & J. Peel, with A. Fabra and R. MacKenzie (eds.), *Principles of International Environmental Law* (3rd edition, Cambridge University Press, 2003).

Soares de Lima, M. R., *The Political Economy of Brazilian Foreign Policy: Nuclear Energy, Trade and Itaipu* (Brasilia: FUNAG, 2013).

Tignino, M., '*Joint Infrastructure and the Sharing of Benefits in the Senegal and Niger Watershed*', 41:6 Water International (2016): 835–850.

Van Loon, H., '*The Global Horizon of Private International Law*', 380 Recueil des Cours (2016): 9–108.

Viceministerio de Minas y Energía, Paraguay. Reseña Energética — Consumo Final de Energía. Sistema de Información Energética Nacional (SIEN) de la Dirección de Recursos Energéticos Primarios del Vice Ministerio de Minas y Energía. Last accessed 14 February 2019.

Viceministerio de Minas y Energía, Paraguay. Balance Energético Nacional 2017, August 2018, at 26. https://www.ssme.gov.py/vmme/pdf/balance2017/BEN2017.pdf (Last accessed 14 February 2019).

Vick, M. J., '*The Senegal River Basin: A Retrospective and Prospective Look at the Legal Regime*', 46 Natural Resources Journal (2006): 211–243.

Waite, G., '*International Law Affecting Water Rights in the Western States*', 4:1 Land and Water Law Review (1969): 67–96.

Wasmosy, J. C., *Archivo Itaipu. Memorias y Documentos Inéditos* (ColorShop Estacion Grafica SRL, 2008).

Zydan Soria, M., *Usina de Itaipu. Integracao Energética Entre Brasil e Paraguai* (Editora UFPR, 2012).

www.ingramcontent.com/pod-product-compliance
Lightning Source LLC
Chambersburg PA
CBHW071356230926
51846CB00002B/573
* 9 7 8 9 0 0 4 4 0 2 0 8 9 *